Management Report: Improvements are Needed to Enhance the Internal Revenue Service's Internal Controls

United States Government Accountability Office
Washington, DC 20548

May 13, 2013

Mr. Steven T. Miller
Acting Commissioner of Internal Revenue

Subject: *Management Report: Improvements Are Needed to Enhance the Internal Revenue Service's Internal Controls*

Dear Mr. Miller:

In November 2012, we issued our report on the results of our audit of the financial statements of the Internal Revenue Service (IRS) as of, and for the fiscal years ending, September 30, 2012, and 2011, and on the effectiveness of its internal control over financial reporting as of September 30, 2012.[1] We also reported our conclusions on IRS's compliance with selected provisions of laws and regulations and on whether IRS's financial management systems substantially comply with the requirements of the Federal Financial Management Improvement Act of 1996. In March 2013, we issued a report on information security issues identified during our fiscal year 2012 audit, along with associated recommendations for corrective actions.[2]

In November 2012, we also issued our report on the results of procedures we agreed to perform for the Department of Transportation's Office of Inspector General concerning the amount of excise tax distributions made to the Airport and Airway Trust Fund and the Highway Trust Fund for the fiscal year ended September 30, 2012.[3] We performed these procedures in conjunction with our fiscal year 2012 IRS financial statement audit procedures.

The purpose of this report is to present internal control deficiencies identified during our audit of IRS's fiscal year 2012 financial statements and our excise tax agreed-upon procedures work for which we did not already have outstanding recommendations. Although most of these deficiencies were not discussed in our report on the results of our fiscal year 2012 financial statement audit

---

[1]GAO, *Financial Audit: IRS's Fiscal Years 2012 and 2011 Financial Statements*, GAO-13-120 (Washington, D.C.: Nov. 9, 2012).

[2]GAO, *Information Security: IRS Has Improved Controls but Needs to Resolve Weaknesses*, GAO-13-350 (Washington, D.C.: Mar. 15, 2013).

[3]GAO, *Fiscal Year 2012 Agreed-Upon Procedures: Excise Tax Distributions to the Airport and Airway Trust Fund and the Highway Trust Fund*, GAO-13-73R (Washington, D.C.: Nov. 7, 2012). The Department of Transportation is the administrator of these two trust funds.

because they were not considered material or significant,[4] and were not reported in our excise tax agreed-upon procedures report, they nonetheless warrant IRS management's attention. This report provides 14 recommendations to address the internal control issues we identified as part of our fiscal year 2012 IRS financial statement audit and agreed-upon procedures. This report also presents the status, as of September 30, 2012, of IRS corrective actions taken to address our 69 previous recommendations that remained open at the end of the fiscal year 2011 audit. These were detailed in a report we issued in June 2012 on the status of IRS's implementation of the recommendations from our prior IRS financial audits and related financial management reports.[5]

Results in Brief

During our audit of IRS's fiscal year 2012 financial statements, we identified the following new internal control deficiency that contributed to our continuing material weakness in internal control over unpaid tax assessments as of September 30, 2012:

- **Unpaid Tax Assessments Estimation Process.** IRS's controls over its process for estimating the balances of federal taxes receivable and other unpaid tax assessments were not effectively implemented to ensure the proper accounting classification and dollar amounts.[6] This deficiency increases the risk that a material misstatement of IRS's financial statements may not be prevented, or detected and corrected, on a timely basis.

In addition, we identified the following less significant, new internal control deficiencies as of September 30, 2012:

- **Refunds Disbursed to Deceased Taxpayers.** IRS's internal controls were not effectively designed to ensure that deceased taxpayers were timely identified in its taxpayer records and that refunds issued to deceased taxpayers were valid. These deficiencies increase IRS's risk of issuing erroneous refunds to deceased taxpayers and fraudulent refunds to identity thieves.

- **Authorization of Manual Refunds.** IRS's procedures were not effectively designed to ensure that those individuals allowed to approve the issuance of manual refunds were

---

[4]A material weakness is a deficiency, or combination of deficiencies, in internal control such that there is a reasonable possibility that a material misstatement of the entity's financial statements will not be prevented, or detected and corrected, on a timely basis. A significant deficiency is a deficiency, or combination of deficiencies, in internal control that is less severe than a material weakness, yet important enough to merit attention by those charged with governance. A deficiency in internal control exists when the design or operation of a control does not allow management or employees, in the normal course of performing their assigned functions, to prevent, or detect and correct, misstatements on a timely basis.

[5]GAO, *Internal Revenue Service: Status of GAO Financial Audit and Related Financial Management Recommendations*, GAO-12-695 (Washington, D.C.: June 28, 2012).

[6]An unpaid tax assessment is a legally enforceable claim against a taxpayer and consists of taxes, penalties, and interest that have not been collected or abated (i.e., the tax assessment reduced by IRS). Federal taxes receivable represents the portion of unpaid assessments that is supported by taxpayer agreement or a favorable court ruling and must be reported on the financial statements.

properly appointed to do so.[7] This deficiency increases the risk that IRS may disburse erroneous or fraudulent manual refunds.

- **Computer System Access Rights of Employees Handling Taxpayer Receipts.** IRS's policies and procedures were not effectively designed to appropriately limit remittance perfection technicians' system access to change taxpayer account information.[8] This deficiency increases the risk that remittance perfection technicians—who have custody of hard-copy taxpayer receipts and taxpayer information—could misappropriate tax payments and alter taxpayer accounts to conceal these acts.

- **Cost Allocation and User Fee Classification for the Statement of Net Cost.** IRS's controls were not effectively designed and implemented to ensure that IRS fully allocated costs or correctly classified all user fee exchange revenue within its Integrated Financial System, which IRS uses to prepare its Statement of Net Cost. This increases the risk of misstatement on its Statement of Net Cost.

- **Recording of Obligation of Funds.** IRS's policies and procedures were not effectively designed to ensure that IRS staff recorded an obligation for goods and services prior to taking delivery of them from a contractor or a performing federal agency. This increases the risk that IRS may violate the Antideficiency Act, which prohibits federal agencies from obligating or spending in excess of their available funding or accepting voluntary services. It also increases the risk that IRS managers may make operating decisions and allocate resources based on incomplete financial data.

- **Excise Tax Receipt Certification Process.** IRS's controls were not effectively implemented to ensure that staff properly calculated the quarterly excise tax revenues to be distributed to the Airport and Airway Trust Fund and the Highway Trust Fund. In addition, IRS's existing procedures were not operating effectively to ensure that changes it made to its methodology for calculating the amount of revenues to be distributed were concurred with by all affected parties within the Department of the Treasury (Treasury) prior to implementing the changes.[9] These deficiencies increase the risk that the amounts IRS certifies for distribution to the trust funds and the amounts that Treasury actually distributes to the trust funds may be incorrect.

This report provides 2 new recommendations pertaining to IRS's continuing material weakness in internal control over unpaid tax assessments and 12 new recommendations related to the other identified control deficiencies, for a total of 14 new recommendations. These recommendations are intended to improve IRS's internal controls over its financial management and accountability of

---

[7]A manual refund is a refund that is not generated by normal computer processing and is therefore subject to manual review.

[8]Remittance perfection technicians are employees who are responsible for researching taxpayer receipts sent to service center campuses that are unaccompanied by supporting documents such as tax returns, vouchers, or other instructions needed to ensure that the receipts are credited to the proper taxpayer, tax period, and tax class.

[9]IRS and other Treasury agencies, including the Office of Tax Analysis and the Financial Management Service, work together to collect and distribute excise taxes to trust funds.

resources as well as bring IRS into conformance with its own policies, the *Standards for Internal Control in the Federal Government*,[10] or both.

As of September 30, 2012, IRS had completed corrective action on 23 of the 69 recommendations from our prior financial audits and other financial management-related work that remained open at the beginning of the fiscal year 2012 financial audit. As a result, IRS currently has 60 recommendations that need to be addressed, which consists of the previous 46 open recommendations as well as the 14 new recommendations we are making in this report.

We provided IRS with a draft of this report and obtained its written comments. In its comments, IRS agreed with all 14 of our new recommendations and described the actions it had taken, had under way, or planned to take to address the control deficiencies described in this report. In addition to its written comments, IRS provided technical comments on a draft of this report, which we incorporated as appropriate. At the end of our discussion of each of the issues in this report, we have summarized IRS's related comments and provided our evaluation. We have reprinted IRS's comments in their entirety in enclosure II.

Scope and Methodology

This report addresses internal control deficiencies we identified during our audit of IRS's fiscal years 2012 and 2011 financial statements and during our agreed-upon procedures work concerning excise tax distributions to the Airport and Airway Trust Fund and the Highway Trust Fund. As part of our financial statement audit, we tested IRS's internal control over financial reporting.[11] We designed our audit procedures to test relevant controls, including those for proper authorization, execution, accounting, and reporting of transactions and for the safeguarding of assets and taxpayer information. In conducting the audit, we reviewed applicable IRS policies and procedures, observed operations, tested samples of transactions, examined relevant documents and records, and interviewed management and staff. Further details on our audit scope and methodology are provided in our November 2012 report on the results of our audit of IRS's fiscal years 2012 and 2011 financial statements.[12]

Our procedures also involved checking the accuracy of the amounts IRS certified for distribution to the Airport and Airway Trust Fund and the Highway Trust Fund and determining whether excise tax transactions recorded in IRS's systems matched supporting documents. Further details on the

---

[10]GAO, *Standards for Internal Control in the Federal Government*, GAO/AIMD-00-21.3.1 (Washington, D.C.: November 1999), contains the internal control standards to be followed by executive agencies in establishing and maintaining systems of internal control as required by 31 U.S.C. § 3512 (c), (d) (commonly referred to as the Federal Managers' Financial Integrity Act of 1982).

[11]An entity's internal control over financial reporting is a process effected by those charged with governance, management, and other personnel, the objectives of which are to provide reasonable assurance that (1) transactions are properly recorded, processed, and summarized to permit the preparation of financial statements in accordance with U.S. generally accepted accounting principles, and assets are safeguarded against loss from unauthorized acquisition, use, or disposition and (2) transactions are executed in accordance with the laws governing the use of budget authority and other laws and regulations that could have a direct and material effect on the financial statements.

[12]See GAO-13-120.

procedures we performed are provided in our November 2012 report on the results of our agreed-upon procedures work.[13]

We performed our audit of IRS's fiscal years 2012 and 2011 financial statements and our agreed-upon procedures engagement on excise taxes in accordance with U.S. generally accepted government auditing standards. We believe that our work provides a reasonable basis for our findings and conclusions in this report.

Unpaid Tax Assessments Estimation Process

During our fiscal year 2012 audit, we identified errors in IRS's unpaid tax assessments estimation process that its internal review procedures did not detect. Specifically, IRS made errors in determining the accounting classification and dollar amounts of individual taxpayer accounts with unpaid tax assessments that are used to derive the taxes receivable balance reported in IRS's financial statements.[14] Further, these errors were not detected by IRS's supervisory review process. Because of the magnitude of these errors, this deficiency contributed to the material weakness in internal control over unpaid tax assessments that we reported in our report on the results of our audit of IRS's fiscal year 2012 financial statements.[15]

As we have reported in our fiscal year 2012 financial audit and in prior years, IRS does not have a detailed listing, or subsidiary ledger, that accurately tracks and accumulates unpaid tax assessments and their status on an ongoing basis. Specifically, IRS's master files are not designed to provide the accurate, complete, and timely transaction-level financial information necessary to enable IRS to reliably classify and report unpaid tax assessment balances for financial reporting.[16] The amount of taxes receivable recorded in the general ledger is determined by computer programs that analyze taxpayer accounts with unpaid tax assessments and classify the accounts into various financial reporting categories in accordance with federal standards.[17] However, the results of this

---

[13]See GAO-13-73R.

[14]Taxpayer accounts are records in IRS's master files containing information on tax assessments, payments, and other information. A taxpayer may have multiple accounts with IRS, each representing a specific tax for a specific tax period. For example, an individual taxpayer may have an account for personal income tax for tax year 2010 and another account for personal income tax for tax year 2011.

[15]See GAO-13-120.

[16]IRS's master files contain detailed records of taxpayer accounts. However, the master files do not contain all the details necessary to properly classify or estimate collectibility for unpaid tax assessment accounts.

[17]Federal accounting standards classify unpaid tax assessments into one of the following three categories for reporting purposes: federal taxes receivable, compliance assessments, and write-offs. Federal taxes receivable are taxes due from taxpayers for which IRS can support the existence of a receivable through taxpayer agreement or a favorable court ruling. Compliance assessments are tax assessments where neither the taxpayer nor the court has affirmed that the amounts are owed. Write-offs represent unpaid tax assessments for which IRS does not expect further collections because of factors such as the taxpayer's death, bankruptcy, or insolvency. Federal accounting standards only require federal taxes receivable, net of an allowance for uncollectible amounts, to be reported on the financial statements. See Statement of Federal Financial Accounting Standards No. 7, *Accounting for Revenue and Other Financing Sources and Concepts for Reconciling Budgetary and Financial Accounting,* May 10, 1996.

analysis contain material inaccuracies because IRS has not written sufficient details into the classification computer programs to allow them to sort through, identify, and analyze all the relevant transaction-level information required for proper classification. Errors in IRS's manual recording of data into taxpayer accounts also contribute to the computer programs' incorrect determination of the classification and amount of unpaid tax assessments. These system limitations and manual processing errors are the primary reasons we have been reporting a long-standing material internal control weakness with respect to IRS's unpaid tax assessments.

To compensate for these deficiencies, IRS applies a statistical sampling and estimation process to the computer-generated classifications of unpaid tax assessments to estimate the dollar amounts for taxes receivable, compliance assessments, and write-offs to be included in its financial statements and related reports. As part of this compensating process, IRS selected statistical samples of taxpayer accounts from the populations of taxes receivable, compliance assessments, and write-offs as classified by its computer programs. For each sampled account, IRS compares information recorded in the taxpayer's account with various supporting documentation such as tax returns, court documents, and IRS examination files. IRS uses this information to either validate the classification and dollar amount determined by its computer programs or record adjustments to the dollar amount of sampled accounts when IRS's manual analysis of the account determines that the computer-classified amount is incorrect. IRS then statistically projects the extent of any such individual adjustments to determine the gross taxes receivable balance to be used for financial reporting. In fiscal year 2012, the process resulted in $14 billion of adjustments to arrive at the gross taxes receivable balance shown on IRS's financial statements. Because of the significance of the dollar amounts involved and the complexity of IRS's compensating estimation process, it is critical that IRS's controls are effective to help ensure the reliability of the process and the accuracy of the results.

However, our audit tests of unpaid tax assessments during this year's audit found several instances involving complex multimillion-dollar accounts in which our calculation of the sampled taxpayer account balance did not agree with IRS's calculation for the same account. Specifically, we reviewed all 86 of IRS's sampled taxpayer accounts classified as taxes receivable with balances equal to or exceeding $32 million and found errors totaling $829 million in 10 of these accounts.[18] Although IRS's evaluation and calculation of each sampled taxpayer account underwent at least one level of supervisory review, IRS's review process did not identify these errors. IRS subsequently made the necessary corrections so that the errors we identified did not affect IRS's statistical projections and the resulting taxes receivable balance shown in its fiscal year 2012 financial statements.

Internal control standards require agencies to implement internal control procedures to provide reasonable assurance of the accurate and timely recording of transactions and events.[19] In addition, the standards require agencies to provide qualified and continual supervision to provide reasonable assurance that internal control objectives are achieved.

---

[18]IRS included all taxpayer accounts with unpaid assessment balances of $32 million and above in its sample, and we included all of those accounts in our testing as well. Consequently, the $829 million represents the total known error for this subpopulation.

[19]GAO/AIMD-00-21.3.1.

The errors we identified occurred in situations involving complex transactions that necessitated certain legal and accounting interpretations in order to properly classify and value the unpaid tax assessment. While IRS has documented guidance for its staff to follow in evaluating the accounting classification and determining the dollar amounts of the sampled accounts, the guidance is not detailed or specific enough to address scenarios in which taxpayer accounts include more complex transactions. Furthermore, IRS's procedures do not require that the sampled accounts be reviewed by management officials above the unit manager, even when the cases are complex. Consequently, in the sample items for which we identified errors, neither the staff performing the account evaluations nor the supervisors reviewing the work were aware that additional factors should have been considered in determining the proper accounting classification and dollar amount of the sampled account. The lack of sufficient guidance and higher levels of management review for evaluating taxpayers accounts that include more complex transactions increases the risk that IRS staff may make errors in determining the classification and dollar amounts of unpaid tax assessments that are used in IRS's compensating statistical estimation process to derive its reported taxes receivable balance. This, in turn, increases the risk that a material misstatement of IRS's taxes receivable balance may be made and not be timely detected and corrected.

Recommendations for Executive Action

We recommend that you direct the appropriate IRS officials to take the following actions with respect to IRS's compensating statistical estimation process for unpaid tax assessments:

- Update the existing guidance for classifying and determining the dollar amount of individual unpaid assessments to provide additional guidance or specific procedures to follow when evaluating taxpayer accounts that involve complex legal and accounting interpretations. In updating the guidance, consider whether additional levels of management review should be performed on such complex cases.

- Provide training on the new guidance to help staff evaluate and determine the proper accounting classification and amount of unpaid tax assessments, and to help with supervisory review of the sampled taxpayer accounts.

Agency Comments and Our Evaluation

IRS agreed with our recommendations and stated that in March 2013, it updated the guidance for classifying and determining the dollar amount of unpaid assessments to provide additional guidance for evaluating taxpayer accounts that involve complex legal and accounting interpretations and to include additional levels of review for such cases. IRS also stated it provided training on the new guidance in March 2013. If effectively implemented, IRS's actions should address the issue that gave rise to our recommendations. We will evaluate the effectiveness of IRS's actions during our audit of its fiscal year 2013 financial statements.

Refunds Disbursed to Deceased Taxpayers

During our fiscal year 2012 financial audit, we found numerous instances in which IRS erroneously disbursed invalid refunds to deceased taxpayers. Specifically, based on a selected sample of 74 refunds disbursed to deceased taxpayers during fiscal year 2012, we found that 65, or approximately 88 percent, were invalid.[20] For example, we found instances in which IRS issued refunds based on an improper tax form; an improper filing status; or unallowable exemptions, standard deductions, or tax credits (such as the Earned Income Tax Credit).[21] We provided these invalid refunds to IRS for investigation and based on its review, IRS concluded that 31 of the 65 invalid refunds appeared to be the result of identity theft.

A surviving spouse or a court-appointed representative is permitted to request a tax refund on behalf of a deceased taxpayer. However, the filing process and required tax form is different after the year of death. For example, a request for a refund for a deceased taxpayer after the year of death must be claimed by filing a Form 1041, U.S. Income Tax Return for Estates and Trusts, rather than filing a Form 1040, U.S. Individual Income Tax Return.

The Social Security Administration (SSA) provides IRS with weekly updates on individual deaths. However, IRS did not have effective controls in place to reasonably ensure that this information was used to reflect the taxpayers' deceased status in its master files. At the time of our review, IRS's procedures for processing refunds to deceased taxpayers relied on the receipt of a final tax return or valid proof of death documentation for staff to manually record an indicator in the taxpayer's master file account to reflect the taxpayer's deceased status. However, until or unless IRS received such documentation validating a taxpayer's death, the taxpayer's account in the master files would show that the taxpayer was not deceased. As a result, IRS was not able to identify invalid tax returns filed against these deceased taxpayer accounts because the master files were not yet updated to reflect their deceased status. This deficiency in controls resulted in the disbursement of invalid refunds to deceased taxpayers and potentially to identity thieves.

Internal control standards state that internal controls should be designed to provide reasonable assurance regarding the prevention of or prompt detection of unauthorized use or disposition of agency assets. This includes providing reasonable assurance that invalid or fraudulent refund disbursements will be prevented or detected. The standards further state that internal controls should generally be designed to ensure that ongoing monitoring occurs in the course of normal operations. Monitoring should be performed continually and be ingrained in the agency's operations. It includes regular management and supervisory activities, comparisons, reconciliations, and other actions people take in performing their duties.

---

[20]The 74 refunds reviewed were selected from a population of 370 refunds that we identified as suspicious based on our comparison of death information IRS received from the Social Security Administration to related tax filing information in IRS's master files. The population of 370 refunds consisted of (1) 338 refunds issued to deceased taxpayers receiving one suspicious refund each, from which we selected a statistical sample of 42 refunds and (2) 32 refunds issued to deceased taxpayers that had received multiple suspicious refunds, from which we selected all of them for review. Based on the statistical sample of 42 refunds, we are 90 percent confident that at least 89 percent of the 338 suspicious refund transactions disbursed to deceased taxpayers resulted in invalid refunds. For the sample of 32 refunds, which was 100 percent of the population of multiple refunds that were disbursed to deceased taxpayers, we identified 30 invalid refunds.

[21]Generally, the rules for exemptions, deductions and tax credits allowed to individual taxpayers also apply to deceased taxpayers when a final tax return (Form 1040, U.S. Individual Income Tax Return) is filed in the year of death. However, in the years subsequent to the deceased taxpayers' year of death, a different tax return (Form 1041, U.S. Income Tax Return for Estates and Trust) is required, and the rules on the eligibility for these exemptions, deductions, and tax credits change. See IRS Publication 559, *Survivors, Executors, and Administrators* (rev. Feb. 8, 2013).

Based on our findings and inquiries concerning invalid tax refunds to deceased taxpayers, IRS subsequently performed a detailed review of the status of taxpayer accounts in its master files to properly identify deceased taxpayers using the SSA information. IRS informed us that based on its review, it identified approximately 11.5 million taxpayer accounts in its master files that had not been updated to show that the taxpayers were deceased. IRS officials informed us that IRS has since recorded an identifier in the affected master file accounts of these taxpayers to indicate their deceased status in order to prevent the improper filing of tax returns and issuance of invalid refunds in the future.

Further, IRS officials stated that IRS is in the process of establishing a computer program that will routinely perform a comparison of date of death information between SSA and the master files. If there is a discrepancy, the computer program will automatically record an indicator to the taxpayer's account in the master files to reflect the deceased status. According to these officials, after the computer program is implemented, tax returns submitted using a deceased taxpayer's Social Security number will be rejected by IRS's automated tax processing system and subjected to further review. If effectively implemented, the computer program should decrease the number of invalid refunds disbursed to deceased taxpayers including those involving identity theft. We plan to review the effectiveness of the design and implementation of the new computer program during our audit of IRS's fiscal year 2013 financial statements.

Recommendation for Executive Action

We recommend that you direct the appropriate IRS officials to finalize implementation of the automated process for (1) routinely updating date of death information and deceased status in the master files using SSA data and (2) preventing automatic processing of a tax return submitted using a deceased taxpayer's Social Security number.

Agency Comments and Our Evaluation

IRS agreed with our recommendation and stated that in January 2013, it implemented programming to provide weekly updates to the master files using data on dates of death provided by the Social Security Administration. These updates cause any tax returns received under the decedent's Social Security number to undergo additional review to ensure any refund claims are appropriate. IRS's actions, if effectively implemented, should address the issue that gave rise to our recommendation. We will evaluate the effectiveness of IRS's efforts during our audit of IRS's fiscal year 2013 financial statements.

Authorization of Manual Refunds

During our fiscal year 2012 financial audit, we found that a program director delegated to a second official the authority to appoint individuals to approve manual refunds; however, the program director did not properly document this delegation of authority. Specifically, we found that the program director did not document the delegation of authority to the second official until after the second official had appointed 29 individuals to sign and approve manual refunds. As a result, the second official appointed these individuals without having the proper documented authority to do so.

IRS disburses most refunds to taxpayers automatically after their tax returns are posted to their master file accounts and any overpayments to IRS are identified and calculated. However, IRS's Internal Revenue Manual (IRM) requires that proposed refunds meeting certain criteria, such as those exceeding $10 million, be manually reviewed and approved before disbursement.[22] IRS refers to these refunds as manual refunds. Because these manual refunds bypass most of the automated validity checks, it is important that those individuals approving such refunds be appropriately appointed and authorized to do so to reduce the risk of approving and disbursing invalid refunds.

The IRM states that heads of office, which IRS defines as executives or directors of program areas, are responsible for appointing authority to specific individuals to sign and authorize manual refunds.[23] The program executives and directors are to document these appointments on a manual refund signature authorization form and forward them to the manual refund unit located at a service center campus (SCC).[24] The IRM also allows a program executive or director to delegate the authority to appoint individuals to serve as approvers of manual refunds to another director or equivalent by completing a designation to act form which is to be maintained on file in the manual refund unit along with the manual refund signature authorization form.[25] Therefore, those who approve manual refunds must be both properly appointed and authorized.

According to the IRM, before processing a manual refund, the manual refund unit is required to verify that the individual who signed and approved the manual refund is authorized to do so by comparing the signature on the manual refund to the signature authorization form. However, at the time of our review IRS did not require the manual refund unit to review the designation to act form where applicable to ensure that the person approving the manual refund had been properly appointed. We found that the manual refund unit at one SCC accepted the manual refund signature authorization forms for 29 individuals to serve as manual refund approvers without a proper designation to act form attached or on file. These 29 individuals had all been appointed by the same delegated official; however, the program director did not sign the designation to act form delegating authority to the second official until after the official had appointed the 29 individuals.

Internal control standards state that transactions and other significant events should be authorized and executed only by persons acting in the scope of their authority to provide reasonable assurance that only valid transactions are authorized, approved, and processed. Authorizations should be clearly communicated to managers and employees.[26] The lack of policies and procedures for ensuring proper delegation of authority for IRS officials appointing individuals to approve manual

---

[22]IRM § 21.4.4.2, *Why Would A Manual Refund Be Needed?* (June 18, 2012). The IRM outlines business rules and administrative procedures and guidelines IRS uses to conduct its operations, and contains policy, direction, and delegations of authority necessary to carry out IRS's responsibilities to administer tax law and other legal provisions.

[23]IRM § 3.17.79.3.5, *Employees Authorized to Sign Requests for Refunds* (Jan. 1, 2012).

[24]Form 14031, Manual Refund Signature Authorization Form, documents the name and signature of the individual authorized to sign and approve manual refunds. SCCs process tax returns and payments submitted by taxpayers.

[25]Form 10247, Designation to Act, is valid in the absence of a director or equivalent.

[26]GAO/AIMD-00-21.3.1.

refunds diminishes the effectiveness of IRS's internal controls over manual refunds, and increases the risk that erroneous or potentially fraudulent refunds may be disbursed.

In January 2013, IRS revised its IRM to require the manual refund unit to ensure that a designation to act form is submitted with the signature authorization form when it is signed by a delegated official, and to review each designation to act form to ensure that the designation date is prior to the signature authorization form's approval date.[27] We will assess the effectiveness of IRS's revised policy during our fiscal year 2013 audit.

Recommendation for Executive Action

We recommend that you direct the appropriate IRS officials to implement the policies and procedures that require the manual refund unit to verify that (1) any manual refund signature authorization forms that are signed by a delegated official are accompanied by a designation to act form, and (2) the designation to act form is dated prior to the approval date on the manual refund signature authorization form.

Agency Comments and Our Evaluation

IRS agreed with our recommendation and stated that, in January 2013, it updated the IRM to require the manual refund unit to verify (1) any manual refund signature authorization forms that are signed by a delegated official are accompanied by a designation to act form, and (2) the designation to act form is dated prior to the approval date on the manual refund signature authorization form. IRS's actions, if effectively implemented, should address the issue that gave rise to our recommendation. We will evaluate the effectiveness of IRS's efforts during our audit of IRS's fiscal year 2013 financial statements.

Computer System Access Rights of Employees Handling Taxpayer Receipts

During our fiscal year 2012 audit, we found that IRS did not appropriately limit the computer access rights of certain employees who had custody of hard-copy receipts and sensitive information from taxpayers.[28] Specifically, we found that remittance perfection technicians at all three SCCs we visited who had custody of hard-copy taxpayer receipts and taxpayer information were also provided unrestricted access to the Integrated Data Retrieval System (IDRS) which can be used to alter taxpayer accounts.[29]

Remittance perfection technicians at SCCs are responsible for researching taxpayer receipts that are unaccompanied by supporting documents such as tax returns, vouchers, or other instructions needed to ensure that the receipts are credited to the proper taxpayer, tax period, and tax class. To

---

[27]IRM § 3.17.79.3.5, *Employees Authorized to Sign Requests for Refunds* (Jan. 18, 2013).

[28]Hard-copy receipts and information refers to checks, money orders, negotiable instruments, tax forms, or other correspondences that IRS does not receive electronically.

[29]IDRS is an IRS computer system that provides employees with the ability to research taxpayer account information; request tax returns and account transcripts; input transactions such as adjustments and entity changes; input collection information for storage and processing in the system; and generate notices, collection documents, and other outputs.

obtain the information needed to process these taxpayer receipts, remittance perfection technicians need limited access to IDRS to allow them to research taxpayer account information. However, we found that remittance perfection technicians instead had unrestricted access to IDRS. Such unrestricted access could also allow them to make unauthorized changes in IDRS to (1) adjust a taxpayer's account balance, (2) change the status of a tax module or taxpayer's account, or (3) change a taxpayer's liability.

We have found similar issues in prior year audits. For example, during our fiscal year 2007 audit, we found that IRS did not always appropriately restrict sensitive IDRS command codes from taxpayer assistance center employees who had the authority to accept cash payments from taxpayers.[30] In addition, during our fiscal year 2011 audit, we found that clerks in the campus support unit had the ability to make adjustments to taxpayer accounts through IDRS while also maintaining physical possession of hard-copy receipts in the course of their payment processing duties.[31] In each of these cases, IRS responded to our findings by updating the IRM and implementing controls to restrict the level of IDRS access for these specific types of employees, but did not undertake a global review of the level of IDRS access provided to all employees who handle hard-copy taxpayer receipts and related sensitive information to ensure their level of IDRS access was appropriate. Consequently, we continue to find classes of employees who both handle hard-copy taxpayer receipts and have the access rights in IDRS to alter taxpayer accounts.

The IRM identifies certain employee groups, such as revenue agents and employees responsible for accepting cash payments, that are to be restricted from having access to sensitive IDRS command codes based on the nature of their work and the risks involved, and provides a list of specific codes that should be restricted from their IDRS profiles.[32] However, at the time of our visits to the SCCs, the IRM did not address any required access restrictions for remittance perfection technicians. In response to our finding, IRS updated the IRM in August 2012 to restrict remittance perfection technicians from having access to all sensitive command codes.[33] However, we found that IRS had not performed a risk assessment to determine the appropriate level of IDRS access required by remittance perfection technicians prior to revising the IRM. Consequently, IRS management later informed us that there were instances where some remittance perfection technicians needed access to certain sensitive command codes as part of their normal job duties, but the IRM did not provide for such exceptions. Further, while IRS updated the IRM, it had not established controls to prevent remittance perfection technicians from gaining access to restricted command codes not needed to perform their assigned duties.

---

[30]GAO, *Management Report: Improvements Needed in IRS's Internal Controls*, GAO-08-368R (Washington, D.C.: June 4, 2008).

[31]GAO, *Management Report: Improvements Are Needed to Enhance the Internal Revenue Service's Internal Controls and Operating Effectiveness*, GAO-12-683R (Washington, D.C.: June 25, 2012).

[32]IRM § 10.8.34, *Information Technology (IT) Security, IDRS Security Controls* (Oct. 14, 2011); IRM Exhibit § 10.8.34-7, *Restricted Command Codes for the Role: Revenue Agents, Tax Compliance Officers, and Estate Tax Attorneys* (Oct. 14, 2011); and IRM Exhibit § 10.8.34-9, *Restricted Command Codes for the Role: 809 Receipt Book Users and Remittance Perfection Technician* (Oct. 14, 2011).

[33]IRM § 3.8.45.1.3.1, *Separation of Duties, Sensitive IDRS Command Codes for Remittance Perfection Technicians* (Aug. 9, 2012).

Internal control standards require controls to protect systems from inappropriate access. Internal control standards also require restrictions that only allow users access to functions that they need to perform their duties. No one individual should have access to a system that allows him or her to both cause and conceal an error or irregularity by controlling certain key aspects of a transaction or event.[34] Without (1) an understanding of the risks posed by allowing remittance perfection technicians to have access to sensitive IDRS command codes or (2) controls that prevent remittance technicians from gaining access to prohibited command codes, IRS cannot be assured that it has properly limited remittance perfection technicians' access to IDRS. This, in turn, increases the risk that remittance perfection technicians could misappropriate tax payments and alter taxpayer accounts to conceal these acts.

Recommendations for Executive Action

We recommend that you direct the appropriate IRS officials to take the following actions:

- Perform a risk assessment to determine the appropriate level of IDRS access that should be granted to employee groups that handle hard-copy taxpayer receipts and related sensitive taxpayer information as part of their job responsibilities.

- Based on the results of the risk assessment, update the IRM accordingly to specify the appropriate level of IDRS access that should be allowed for (1) remittance perfection technicians and (2) all other employee groups with IDRS access that handle hard-copy taxpayer receipts and related sensitive information as part of their job responsibilities.

- Establish procedures to implement the updated IRM, including required steps to follow to prevent (1) remittance perfection technicians and (2) all other employee groups that handle hard-copy taxpayer receipts and related sensitive information as part of their job responsibilities from gaining access to command codes not required as part of their designated job duties.

Agency Comments and Our Evaluation

IRS agreed with our recommendations and stated that by October 2014, it will perform a risk assessment to determine the appropriate level of IDRS access that should be granted to employees who handle hard-copy taxpayer receipts and related sensitive taxpayer information. IRS also stated that by December 2015, it will update the IRM to specify the appropriate levels of IDRS access based on the risk assessment results, evaluate existing controls that prevent employees from gaining access to command codes not required for their job duties, and establish additional procedures as necessary. IRS's actions, if effectively implemented, should address the issue that gave rise to our recommendations. We will evaluate the effectiveness of IRS's efforts during future audits of IRS's financial statements.

Cost Allocation and User Fee Classification for the Statement of Net Cost

During our fiscal year 2012 financial audit, we found that IRS did not fully allocate costs or correctly classify user fees within its Integrated Financial System (IFS), which IRS uses to prepare its

---

[34] GAO/AIMD-00-21.3.1.

Statement of Net Cost.[35] The Statement of Net Cost, one of the basic federal financial statements, is designed to show the net cost of operations for the reporting entity as a whole, by major program. Certain costs, such as the salaries of staff members who work directly for those programs, are easily identified by program. However, many costs, such as costs of rent and facilities, technology support, and payroll operations, support multiple programs and must therefore be allocated in order to fairly report all relevant program costs on the Statement of Net Cost.

IRS uses a combination of monthly automated and manual processes to collect and prepare cost data, including over 600 computerized commands to allocate indirect costs to its direct business units.[36] To help ensure that all costs were properly allocated, IRS cost accountants are required to run and review edit checks within IFS to detect any support costs that were not allocated to the direct business units. If any unallocated costs remain, the cost accountants are to design and execute additional actions to allocate them. The cost accountants then run a report that IRS uses either to verify that all costs were allocated as intended or, if they were not, to take additional action as needed to allocate the remaining unallocated costs.

User fees do not go through the allocation process. Instead, they are classified on the Statement of Net Cost by major program based on the functional area (for example, Media and Publications or Submission Processing) to which they are assigned.[37] Consequently, the accurate classification of user fees on the Statement of Net Cost depends, in part, on IRS staff assigning the correct functional area codes in IFS when posting user fee transactions.

In our review of IRS's draft Statement of Net Cost, we noted the following two instances in which costs were not fully allocated or user fees were incorrectly classified.

- IRS did not allocate about $2.3 million of costs to any of the direct business units during the year-end cost allocation process as required. This occurred because two controls did not detect these unallocated costs. First, an edit check showed zero unallocated costs remained because IRS erroneously included a revenue account in the cost allocation process that when offset against the $2.3 million of unallocated costs, resulted in a $0 net balance. Had the revenue account not been included to erroneously offset the unallocated costs, the edit check would have identified the problem. Second, IRS staff ran a report at the end of the allocation that showed that there were unallocated costs remaining, but IRS staff were unaware that any unallocated costs existed until we brought this issue to their attention. IRS staff informed us that although they had reviewed the report, which they call the

---

[35]IFS is IRS's administrative accounting system which IRS uses to record, classify, summarize, and report financial transactions and prepare its financial statements.

[36]In this context, we are defining indirect costs as those costs that do not directly correlate to one of the direct business units that IRS identifies as falling in line with its overall function. These units are Wage and Investment, Large Business and International, Small Business/Self Employed, Tax Exempt and Government Entities, and Criminal Investigation.

[37]A functional area identifies a group of activities related to a specific function. Functional area codes are used for internal management and financial planning purposes, as well as for classifying costs on the Statement of Net Cost.

Presentation 1.1 report, they did not notice the unallocated costs during their review.[38] IRS's written procedures require reviewing this report to compare total costs to the trial balance and other financial reports, but do not require reviewing it to verify that all indirect costs were allocated to the direct business units. Because the total costs on the report included the $2.3 million of unallocated costs, IRS's total costs still reconciled. IRS should have allocated these costs to the Criminal Investigation Division; by not doing so, this resulted in that business unit's total costs being understated. Nevertheless, because the $2.3 million of unallocated costs was aligned with IRS's compliance program, for which Criminal Investigation Division costs are also aligned, no adjustment to the Statement of Net Cost was necessary. However, had the unallocated costs aligned to a different program, IRS's program costs reported on its Statement of Net Cost would have been misstated.

- IRS did not correctly classify Special Enrollment Exam User Fee revenue collected during at least the first 6 months of fiscal year 2012. Specifically, we reviewed IRS's user fee classifications as of March 31, 2012, and found almost $123,000 of the nearly $159,000 collected to date from this user fee was assigned an incorrect accounting code. This occurred because staff from IRS's Office of Cost Accounting changed the functional area code assigned to the user fee but did not notify staff from the Debt Collection Unit, who record user fee transactions, of the change. IRS did not have procedures requiring that Debt Collection Unit staff be timely notified of any changes to assigned codes. Consequently, the error went undetected until August 2012. This error caused Compliance program revenues to be understated and Taxpayer Assistance and Education program revenues to be overstated by over $122,000. IRS corrected the error so that it did not affect its year-end Statement of Net Cost.

Internal control standards require that agencies (1) implement internal control procedures to ensure the accurate and timely recording of transactions and events, (2) promptly record transactions to maintain their relevance and value to management in controlling operations and making decisions, (3) have both operational and financial data in order to achieve their control objectives and help management ensure the effective and efficient use of resources, and (4) clearly document internal controls and all transactions and have the documentation readily available for examination.[39] By not completely allocating costs and accurately classifying user fee revenue to the correct major program, IRS risks presenting inaccurate information on its Statement of Net Cost. In addition, without accurate cost accounting information, IRS's ability to use the data as a decision-making tool is hindered.

Recommendations for Executive Action

We recommend that you direct the appropriate IRS officials to take the following actions:

- Establish and implement written procedures to ensure that only costs are included in the cost allocation process.

---

[38]After all indirect costs have been allocated, IRS arrays the cost data in multiple report formats for internal management purposes. The Presentation 1.1 report format shows costs by major program and business unit.

[39]GAO/AIMD-00-21.3.1.

- Revise existing procedures to require staff responsible for monitoring the cost allocation to review the Presentation 1.1 report to determine if costs were fully allocated to the direct business units and if not, to allocate the remaining costs.

- Establish and implement written procedures to require that the Office of Cost Accounting inform the Debt Collection Unit of any changes to assigned functional area codes to be used for posting user fee transactions in IFS.

Agency Comments and Our Evaluation

IRS agreed with our recommendations and stated that by June 2013, it will establish and implement written procedures to ensure that only costs are included in the cost allocation process, and will revise existing procedures to require the review of Presentation 1.1 to include identifying that all costs are fully allocated. Additionally, IRS stated it revised its User Fee procedures in November 2012 to require timely notification to the Debt Collection Unit of any changes to the functional area codes and established a procedure to provide a functional area certification listing to the Debt Collection Unit annually. IRS's actions, if effectively implemented, should address the issue that gave rise to our recommendations. We will evaluate the effectiveness of IRS's efforts during our audit of IRS's fiscal year 2013 financial statements.

Recording of Obligation of Funds

During our fiscal year 2012 financial audit, we found that IRS did not always record an obligation for goods or services in its accounting system prior to taking delivery of them from a contractor or a performing federal agency.[40] The Antideficiency Act prohibits federal employees from making or authorizing an obligation or expenditure in excess of the appropriated funds available or from accepting voluntary services.[41] Federal agencies are required to properly record a valid obligation, which serves, in part, to help ensure compliance with the Antideficiency Act.

During our testing of a statistical sample of 86 nonpayroll expenses, we identified seven instances in which IRS did not record an obligation in IFS prior to taking delivery of services from a contractor or a performing federal agency.[42] In four of these instances, IRS began receiving services from contractors before recording an obligation in IFS. In the three remaining instances, IRS received services from a performing federal agency and paid for those services before recording an obligation in IFS. Failure to record an obligation prior to taking delivery of services increases IRS's risk that it will not have sufficient funds available to pay the contractor or the performing federal

---

[40]The scope of our work did not include examining the underlying contracts and interagency agreements to make a legal determination regarding whether IRS complied with all applicable fiscal law provisions.

[41]See the Antideficiency Act, which is codified, as amended, in part at 31 U.S.C. §§ 1341, 1342.

[42]We identified these seven instances during our testing of a statistical sample of 86 transactions covering expenses recorded from October 1, 2011, through May 31, 2012. These included transactions based on both contracts with private vendors and interagency agreements with federal performing agencies. Based on our testing results, we estimate that the value of such expenses that could have the same control error could be as high as $262.6 million (i.e., the net upper error limit at a 95 percent confidence level) out of a population of $2.1 billion.

agency and thereby increases IRS's risk of violating the Antideficiency Act. However, IRS did not have a policy requiring staff to record an obligation before receiving goods or services.

Internal control standards state that transactions should be promptly recorded to maintain their relevance and value to management in controlling operations and making decisions. This applies to the entire process or life cycle of a transaction or event from the initiation and authorization through its final classification in summary records. The standards further state that program managers need both operational and financial data to determine whether they are meeting their agencies' strategic and annual performance plans and meeting their goals for accountability for effective and efficient use of resources. Financial information is required to develop financial statements and, on a day-to-day basis, to make operating decisions and allocate resources.[43] Recording obligations after taking delivery of goods and services increases the risk that managers may make operating decisions and allocate resources based on incomplete financial data.

Recommendation for Executive Action

We recommend that you direct the appropriate IRS officials to establish and implement written policies or procedures that require the agency to record the obligation of funds when a contract or agreement is entered into and prior to taking delivery of goods or services.

Agency Comments and Our Evaluation

IRS agreed with our recommendation and stated that by August 2013, it will update its policies and procedures to require staff to timely record the obligation of funds. IRS's actions, if effectively implemented, should address the issue that gave rise to our recommendation. We will evaluate the effectiveness of IRS's efforts during our audit of IRS's fiscal year 2013 financial statements.

Excise Tax Receipt Certification Process

During fiscal year 2012, we found that IRS made errors in calculating and certifying the amount of quarterly excise tax revenues to be distributed to the Airport and Airway Trust Fund (AATF) and the Highway Trust Fund (HTF), which are administered by the Department of Transportation (Transportation). IRS and other components of Treasury are responsible for collecting and distributing excise tax receipts to these government trust funds. Specifically, Treasury's Office of Tax Analysis (OTA) prepares semimonthly estimates of the amount of excise taxes that should be distributed to the trust funds based on historical IRS certification data and actual total current excise tax revenue collections. Treasury's Financial Management Service uses these estimates to make initial distributions to the trust funds. Subsequent to this initial distribution, IRS certifies quarterly the amounts that should have been distributed to the trust funds based on the tax returns it received, and the Financial Management Service then adjusts the initial distributions to match the certified amount. Consequently, IRS plays a critical role in this process by determining and certifying the amount of excise tax collections that should be distributed to the trust funds each quarter. In addition, IRS must effectively coordinate with the other Treasury agencies that are involved in order to ensure that correct amounts are distributed to the trust funds. Transportation relies on Treasury's procedures and controls to ensure that these billions of dollars in excise taxes are appropriately distributed.

---

[43]GAO/AIMD-00-21.3.1.

For fiscal year 2012, the HTF received about $42.5 billion in excise tax revenues and the AATF received about $12.5 billion. However, in reviewing IRS's excise tax certifications to these trust funds for fiscal year 2012, we found the following.

- **Errors in excise tax calculations.** IRS staff made multiple errors in calculating the excise tax amounts certified to the trust funds that were not detected by supervisory reviews. For example, for the quarter ended March 31, 2012, IRS added $138 million in kerosene credits to the amount certified to the HTF when it should have subtracted $166 million. In another example, IRS erroneously omitted $3 million in collections from its certification to the AATF for the quarter ended June 30, 2012. IRS did not identify or correct these errors until after we or Transportation officials brought them to its attention. These errors occurred in part because IRS did not provide the staff assigned responsibility for performing the excise tax certifications with any comprehensive formal training on the excise tax certification process, despite the complex combination of manual and automated procedures to be followed. Additionally, while IRS had procedures requiring supervisory review of its excise tax certifications and documented that the reviews were performed, the reviewers did not detect the errors we found.

- **Lack of concurrence with change in methodology.** IRS made a significant procedural change without documenting agreement with the various agencies involved within Treasury. Specifically, IRS accelerated the recognition of heavy vehicle use taxes in its certification to the HTF by 3 months. IRS officials stated that they made this change to better match the availability of information needed to classify this type of tax. According to IRS, it had discussed the change with OTA and obtained its concurrence before implementation. However, IRS did not document this concurrence and OTA did not adjust its calculations accordingly, which could have resulted in Treasury erroneously transferring about $800 million more than it should to the HTF during the fourth quarter of fiscal year 2012. Because we brought this to IRS's and OTA's attention before the transfers occurred, there was no effect on excise tax distributions to the HTF for fiscal year 2012. IRS subsequently changed its procedures for certifying heavy vehicle use taxes back to the previous approach.

Internal control standards require agencies to implement internal control procedures to ensure the accurate and timely recording of transactions and events.[44] The standards also require that agency management (1) identify appropriate knowledge and skills needed for various jobs and provide needed training and (2) ensure that there are adequate means of communicating with, and obtaining information from, external stakeholders that may have a significant impact on the agency's achieving its goals. By not ensuring that (1) staff and supervisors responsible for preparing and reviewing the excise tax calculations fully understand IRS's methodology and (2) methodological changes are agreed to and consistently carried out by all affected parties, IRS increases the risk that the amounts it certifies for distribution to the trust funds and therefore the amounts that Treasury ultimately distributes to the trust funds may be incorrect.

---

[44]GAO/AIMD-00-21.3.1.

Recommendations for Executive Action

We recommend that you direct the appropriate IRS officials to take the following actions:

- Develop and implement a formal training program for staff assigned to perform and review excise tax certifications, including a comprehensive step-by-step description of the excise tax certification process.

- Review existing supervisory review procedures to identify and implement additional needed actions to better ensure that certification errors do not continue to go undetected.

- Develop and implement written procedures requiring IRS to obtain documented concurrence from the other Treasury agencies involved in the excise tax collection and distribution process of any changes affecting how IRS calculates the amount of excise taxes it certifies to trust funds before IRS implements the change to its excise tax certification process.

Agency Comments and Our Evaluation

IRS agreed with our recommendations and stated that by May 2013, it will develop and implement formal training for all staff assigned to prepare and review excise tax certifications and implement expanded certification check sheets to enable a more comprehensive supervisory review. Additionally, IRS stated that by January 2014, it will update the IRM to require the agency to obtain documented concurrence from affected Treasury organizations before implementing any changes to how IRS calculates the amount of excise taxes it certifies to the trust funds. IRS's actions, if effectively implemented, should address the issue that gave rise to our recommendations. We will evaluate the effectiveness of IRS's efforts during our audit of IRS's fiscal year 2013 financial statements.

Status of Open Recommendations

IRS has continued to work to address many of the control deficiencies related to open recommendations from our prior financial audits and other financial management-related work.[45] At the beginning of our fiscal year 2012 financial audit, there were 69 recommendations to improve IRS's financial operations and internal controls from prior year audits that we reported as open in our status of recommendations report issued in June 2012.[46] In the course of performing our fiscal year 2012 financial audit, we identified numerous actions IRS took to address many of its previously identified control deficiencies. On the basis of IRS's actions, which we were able to substantiate through our audit, we are closing 23 of these recommendations. Consequently, a total of 60 financial management-related recommendations need to be addressed—46 remaining from our prior years' audits and the 14 new recommendations we are making in this report. See enclosure I for more details on our assessment of the status of IRS's actions to address our prior year recommendations.

---

[45]This does not include information systems security recommendations reported separately and with limited distribution because of their sensitive nature. See GAO-13-350.

[46]GAO-12-695.

- - - -

This report contains recommendations to you. The head of a federal agency is required by 31 U.S.C. § 720 to submit a written statement on actions taken on these recommendations. You should submit your statement to the Senate Committee on Homeland Security and Governmental Affairs and to the House Committee on Oversight and Government Reform within 60 days of the date of this report. A written statement must also be sent to the House and Senate Committees on Appropriations with the agency's first request for appropriations made more than 60 days after the date of this report. Furthermore, to ensure that GAO has accurate, up-to-date information on the status of your agency's actions on our recommendations, we request that you also provide us with a copy of your agency's statement of actions taken on open recommendations. Please send your statement of actions to me or Doreen Eng, Assistant Director, at engd@gao.gov.

This report is intended for use by the management of IRS. We are sending copies to the Chairmen and Ranking Members of the Senate Committee on Appropriations; Senate Committee on Finance; Senate Committee on Homeland Security and Governmental Affairs; House Committee on Appropriations; House Committee on Ways and Means; and House Committee on Oversight and Government Reform, and to the Chairman and Vice-Chairman of the Senate Joint Committee on Taxation. We are also sending copies to the Secretary of the Treasury, the Acting Director of the Office of Management and Budget, and the Chairman of the IRS Oversight Board. In addition, the report is available at no charge on GAO's website at http://www.gao.gov.

We acknowledge and appreciate the cooperation and assistance provided by IRS officials and staff during our audits of IRS's fiscal years 2012 and 2011 financial statements. Please contact me at (202) 512-9377 or clarkce@gao.gov if you or your staff have any questions concerning this report. Contact points for our Offices of Congressional Relations and Public Affairs may be found on the last page of this report. GAO staff who made major contributions to this report are listed in enclosure III.

Sincerely yours,

Cheryl E. Clark

Cheryl E. Clark
Director
Financial Management and Assurance

Enclosures – 3

Enclosure I: Status of Recommendations That Were Open at the Beginning of GAO's Audit of IRS's Fiscal Year 2012 Financial Statements

ID no.	Recommendation	Status
	GAO/AIMD-99-16[47]	
Controls Over Unpaid Tax Assessments - Trust Fund Recovery Penalty		
99-01	Manually review and eliminate duplicate or other assessments that have already been paid off to assure that all accounts related to a single assessment are appropriately credited for payments received. **Action taken:** IRS continues to take corrective actions to address the underlying cause for inaccurate taxpayer account balances caused by not appropriately crediting Trust Fund Recovery Penalty (TFRP) payments to all parties. However, IRS's own testing as well as our testing during fiscal year 2012 continued to find errors and delays in recording and crediting TFRP payments to all related parties, resulting in inaccurate account balances in IRS's systems. By October 2014, IRS plans to complete additional actions to ensure that all accounts related to a single assessment are appropriately credited for payments received.	Open
	GAO-01-42[48]	
Controls Over Release of Tax Liens		
01-06	Implement procedures to closely monitor the release of tax liens to ensure that they are released within 30 days of the date the related tax liability is fully satisfied. As part of these procedures, IRS should carefully analyze the causes of the delays in releasing tax liens identified by our work and prior work by IRS's former internal audit function and ensure that such procedures effectively address these issues. **Action taken:** IRS has taken a number of actions over the years to improve its lien release processing, including the creation of a comprehensive action plan to address the various causes for lien release delays, system enhancements to improve the timeliness of recognizing when a taxpayer has fully satisfied the outstanding tax liability, and periodic testing to evaluate the timeliness of its release of tax liens. However, IRS's own testing in fiscal year 2012 revealed continuing deficiencies in controls pertaining to tax liens associated with insolvency cases, which continue to result in the untimely release of liens. By December 2013, IRS plans to implement additional actions, as necessary, to address the causes of late lien releases on insolvency cases.	Open

---

[47]GAO, *Internal Revenue Service: Immediate and Long-Term Actions Needed to Improve Financial Management*, GAO/AIMD-99-16 (Washington, D.C.: Oct. 30, 1998).

[48]GAO, *Internal Revenue Service: Recommendations to Improve Financial and Operational Management*, GAO-01-42 (Washington, D.C.: Nov. 17, 2000).

ID no.	Recommendation	Status
	GAO-05-247R[49]	

Controls Over Transmittal of Taxpayer Receipts and Information

ID no.	Recommendation	Status
05-33	Enforce the requirement that a document transmittal form listing the enclosed Daily Report of Collection Activity forms be included in transmittal packages, using such methods as more frequent inspections or increased reliance on error reports compiled by the service center teller units receiving the information. **Action taken:** IRS's efforts to address this recommendation are ongoing. IRS reported that it is performing a review in three collection field areas to assess their use of the document transmittal Form 3210 to ensure compliance with the Internal Revenue Manual (IRM). By October 2014, IRS plans to use the results of this review to determine further actions that may be needed to close this recommendation.	Open

Controls Over Manual Refunds

ID no.	Recommendation	Status
05-38	Enforce requirements for monitoring accounts and reviewing monitoring of accounts for manual refunds. **Action taken:** IRS's actions to address this recommendation are ongoing. IRS reported that it is conducting reviews of the refund monitoring process, and has updated its training and guidance in the IRM to address required refund monitoring. However, during our fiscal year 2012 audit, we continued to find instances in which manual refund accounts were not monitored as required by the IRM. We also found that supervisors did not always verify that manual refund initiators or those responsible for centralized monitoring were following proper procedures for monitoring manual refunds.	Open
05-39	Enforce requirements for documenting monitoring actions and supervisory review for manual refunds. **Action taken:** IRS's actions to address this recommendation are ongoing. IRS reported that it is conducting sample reviews and addressing the causes of any documentation lapses, clarifying supervisor review guidance, and emphasizing training for managers and staff. However, during our fiscal year 2012 audit, we continued to find instances where IRS did not document monitoring actions and did not perform supervisory review for manual refunds.	Open

---

[49]GAO, *IRS Management Report: Improvements Needed in IRS's Internal Controls*, GAO-05-247R (Washington, D.C.: Apr. 27, 2005).

ID no.	Recommendation	Status
	GAO-06-543R[50]	

Controls Over Transmittal of Taxpayer Receipts and Information

ID no.	Recommendation	Status
06-02	Enforce compliance with existing requirements that all IRS units transmitting taxpayer receipts and information from one IRS facility to another, including service center campuses, taxpayer assistance centers (TAC), and units within the Large Business and International and the Tax Exempt and Government Entities business operating units, establish a system to track acknowledged copies of document transmittals. **Action taken:** During fiscal year 2012, IRS updated guidance on the use of TAC Follow-up Review Logs used for tracking acknowledged/unacknowledged document transmittal forms. However, at several of the TACs we visited during our fiscal year 2012 audit, we continued to find issues with incomplete or inaccurate tracking of transmittals of documentation. IRS plans to continue TAC reviews through September 2013 to enforce completion of the logs.	Open

Controls Over Physical Security

ID no.	Recommendation	Status
06-05	Equip all taxpayer assistance centers (TAC) with adequate physical security controls to deter and prevent unauthorized access to restricted areas or office space occupied by other IRS units, including those TACs that are not scheduled to be reconfigured to the "new TAC" model in the near future. This includes appropriately separating customer service waiting areas from restricted areas in the near future by physical barriers, such as locked doors marked with signs barring entrance by unescorted customers. **Action taken:** IRS stated that it continues to use several solutions to help secure non-model TACs, including using theater rope or other barriers, signage, and other minor alterations. IRS also stated that it continues to identify priority locations for TAC model build out by evaluating TAC sites and customer feedback. Priority status goes to sites with security, safety and environmental health concerns. Of the 397 TAC locations, IRS stated that 293 have the model TAC with another 10 scheduled for completion prior to the 2013 filing season. IRS plans to continue to build out all TACs in compliance with the security guidelines by October 2014. However, IRS reports that this action is highly dependent on continued funding and overcoming scheduling complexities.	Open

---

[50]GAO, *IRS Management Report: Improvements Needed in IRS's Internal Controls*, GAO-06-543R (Washington, D.C.: May 12, 2006).

ID no.	Recommendation	Status
	GAO-07-689R[51]	
07-04	Develop and implement appropriate corrective actions for any gaps in closed circuit television (CCTV) camera coverage that do not provide an unobstructed view of the entire exterior of the service center campus's perimeter, such as adding or repositioning existing CCTV cameras or removing obstructions. **Action taken:** IRS required that each service center campus perform and validate completion of an assessment of its CCTV system to ascertain if it provided an unobstructed view of the exterior of the campus perimeter. IRS also instituted periodic monitoring controls to assess related CCTV camera coverage weaknesses.	Closed
Controls over Manual Refunds		
07-08	Require that managers or supervisors provide the manual refund initiators in their units with training on the most current requirements to help ensure that they fulfill their responsibilities to monitor manual refunds and document their monitoring actions to prevent the issuance of duplicate refunds. **Action taken:** IRS provided training to affected employees on monitoring manual refunds and performs quarterly checks to ensure that employees with manual refund Integrated Data Retrieval System command codes complete the training. However, during our fiscal year 2012 audit, we found instances in which the manual refund training material was inconsistent with the procedures for manual refund processing. We also found some cases where the manual refund initiators did not complete the required training. We will continue to evaluate the effectiveness of IRS's corrective actions during our fiscal year 2013 audit.	Open

---

[51]GAO, *Management Report: Improvements Needed in IRS's Internal Controls*, GAO-07-689R (Washington, D.C.: May 11, 2007).

ID no.	Recommendation	Status
	GAO-08-368R[52]	

Controls Over Tax Penalty Assessments

| 08-06 | In instances where computer programs that control penalty assessments are not functioning in accordance with the intent of the Internal Revenue Manual (IRM), take appropriate action to correct the programs so that they function in accordance with the IRM.

Action taken: IRS continues to make progress in correcting the programming issues it identified. However, IRS continues to find inaccurate penalty and interest calculations and assessments. IRS fixed some minor errors being tracked by its Penalty and Interest Working Group. However, IRS reported that the lack of programming resources has required it to refocus its efforts in addressing this recommendation. Specifically, IRS reported that it had to incorporate the necessary changes to correct these problems into the Transition State 2 Common Module work targeted for initial release and testing in 2014. IRS reported that it expects to complete its corrective action by September 2014. | Open |

Controls Over Contractor Access to Sensitive Information

| 08-14 | Revise the Internal Revenue Manual (IRM) to include a requirement that IRS conduct periodic, unannounced inspections at off-site contractor facilities entrusted with sensitive IRS information; document the results, including identification of any security issues; and verify that the contractor has taken appropriate corrective actions on any security issues observed.

Action taken: IRS has updated the IRM to require that IRS personnel conduct periodic, unannounced inspections at off-site contractor facilities entrusted with sensitive IRS information and that the results of the inspections be documented. | Closed |

---

[52]GAO, *Management Report: Improvements Needed in IRS's Internal Controls*, GAO-08-368R (Washington, D.C.: June 4, 2008).

ID no.	Recommendation	Status
	GAO-09-513R[53]	

Controls over Couriers

| 09-03 | Document in the Internal Revenue Manual (IRM) minimum requirements for establishing criteria for time discrepancies or other inconsistencies, which if noted as part of the required monitoring of Form 10160, Receipt for Transport of IRS Deposit, would require off-site surveillance of couriers.

Action taken: IRS planned to document the methodology used to determine courier timeframes for delivery of deposits in IRM 3.8.45.1.9.7(3), *Headquarters Deposit Analyst Responsibility*, and in the couriers' statement of work to strengthen oversight controls, by December 2012. We will evaluate IRS's actions to address this recommendation during our fiscal year 2013 audit. | Open |

Controls over Tax Receipts Tracking

| 09-05 | Establish procedures to track and routinely report the total dollar amounts and volumes of receipts collected by individual taxpayer assistance center location, group, territory, area, and nationwide.

Action taken: IRS stated that it completed testing in September 2012 on the use of electronic Form 795A, Remittance and Return Report, to track and report the total dollar amounts and volumes of receipts. Form 795A is accessed through the Accounts Management System (AMS) which allows access to individual group, territory, area, and national level totals. Additionally, IRS plans to update IRM 21.3.4.7.3, *Form 795-A, Remittance and Return Report*, to mandate the use of the Form 795A through AMS. We will evaluate IRS's actions to address this recommendation during our fiscal year 2013 audit. | Open |

---

[53]GAO, *Management Report: Improvements Needed to Enhance IRS's Internal Controls and Operating Effectiveness*, GAO-09-513R (Washington, D.C.: June 24, 2009).

ID no.	Recommendation	Status
Controls Over Physical Security - Alarms		
09-06	Establish procedures to ensure that an inventory of all duress alarms is documented for each location and is readily available to individuals conducting duress alarm tests before each test is conducted. **Action taken:** IRS reported that in October 2012, it updated Standard Operating Procedure SOP-12-0004, *Duress Alarm Test Conducting and Reporting*. The revised procedure requires that an inventory of all duress alarms be documented for each location and be readily available to individuals performing duress alarm tests before each test is conducted. However, the action occurred after September 2012. We will evaluate IRS's actions to address this recommendation during our fiscal year 2013 audit.	Open
09-07	Establish procedures to periodically update the inventory of duress alarms at each taxpayer assistance center location to ensure that the inventory is current and complete as of the testing date. **Action taken:** IRS reported that in October 2012, it updated Standard Operating Procedure SOP-12-0004, *Duress Alarm Test Conducting and Reporting*. The revised procedure requires semiannual validation of alarm inventory to ensure that the inventory is current and complete as of the testing date. However, the action occurred after September 2012. We will evaluate IRS's actions to address this recommendation during our fiscal year 2013 audit.	Open
09-08	Provide instructions for conducting quarterly duress alarm tests to ensure that IRS officials conducting the test (1) document the test results for each duress alarm listed in the inventory, including date, findings, and planned corrective action and (2) track the findings until they are properly resolved. **Action taken:** IRS reported that in October 2012, it updated Standard Operating Procedure SOP-12-0004, *Duress Alarm Test Conducting and Reporting*. The revised procedure provides instructions for performing quarterly duress alarm tests to ensure that officials performing the test (1) document the test results for each duress alarm listed in the inventory, including date, findings, and planned corrective actions, and (2) track the findings until they are properly resolved. However, the action occurred after September 2012. We will evaluate IRS's actions to address this recommendation during our fiscal year 2013 audit.	Open

ID no.	Recommendation	Status
09-09	Establish procedures requiring that each physical security analyst conduct a periodic documented review of the Emergency Signal History Report and emergency contact list for its respective location to ensure that (1) appropriate corrective actions have been planned for all incidents reported by the central monitoring station and (2) the emergency contact list for each location is current and includes only appropriate contacts. **Action taken:** IRS reported that in October 2012, it updated its Standard Operating Procedure SOP-12-0004, *Duress Alarm Test Conducting and Reporting*, to reinforce the requirement that Emergency Signal History Reports be provided monthly to each territory manager for his/her accounts for periodic review. Physical security and emergency preparedness specialists now review the reports, sign and date them, and provide them to the territory manager monthly. The territory manager then reviews the reports to ensure that the appropriate corrective actions have been planned for all incidents reported by central monitoring. IRS reported that the emergency contact list will be updated as changes occur and the Subscriber Detail Report will be reviewed semiannually to ensure the accuracy of the emergency contact list. However, since the action occurred after September 2012, we will evaluate IRS's actions to address this recommendation during our fiscal year 2013 audit.	Open
Controls Over Performance Measurement - Enforcement Activities		
09-16	Develop outcome-oriented performance measures and related performance goals for IRS's enforcement programs and activities that include measures of the full cost of, and the revenue collected from, those programs and activities (return on investment) to assist IRS's managers in optimizing resource allocation decisions and evaluating the effectiveness of their activities. **Action taken:** IRS has continued to improve its ability to measure performance, including measures of return on investment (ROI). IRS has developed a process to capture full cost and revenue information and designed a methodology for calculating ROI information for a variety of its enforcement programs and activities, including the Automated Underreporter, the Automated Collection System, the Automated Substitute for Return, and several other enforcement activities. In fiscal year 2011, IRS began to calculate the actual ROIs for major enforcement programs related to prior enforcement initiatives for which it had developed prospective ROIs in prior year funding requests. In fiscal year 2012, IRS added ROI information for its Balance Due Notice program, which included ROI information on the various notice letters sent to taxpayers. IRS's business unit responsible for the Balance Due Notice Process has begun using the ROI information in its effort to redesign the notice letters and in making decisions about how to most effectively use the letters.	Closed

ID no.	Recommendation	Status
	GAO-10-565R[54]	

Controls Over Unpaid Tax Assessments – Financial Reporting

ID no.	Recommendation	Status
10-01	Review the results of IRS's unpaid tax assessments compensating statistical estimation process to identify and document instances where systemic limitations in the Custodial Detail Data Base (CDDB) resulted in misclassifications of account balances that, in turn, resulted in material inaccuracies in the amounts of reported unpaid assessments. **Action taken:** IRS has identified specific account modules that were misclassified as a result of systemic limitations. However, it has not yet documented the various systemic limitations in CDDB that cause the misclassification of account balances. During our fiscal year 2012 audit, we and IRS continued to identify misclassified unpaid assessments account modules resulting from CDDB systemic limitations. These CDDB limitations caused IRS to record multibillion-dollar adjustments to the year-end CDDB-generated gross taxes receivable balance in order to produce a reliable number for external reporting on its balance sheet for fiscal year 2012.	Open
10-02	Research and implement programming changes to allow Custodial Detail Data Base (CDDB) to more accurately classify such accounts among the three categories of unpaid tax assessments. **Action taken:** In June 2012, IRS implemented a programming change in CDDB to accurately classify unpaid tax assessments related to individual taxpayers for modules with split classifications between taxes receivable and compliance assessments. IRS plans to implement a similar programming change for business taxpayers by September 2013.	Open
10-03	Research and identify control weaknesses resulting in inaccuracies or errors in taxpayer accounts that materially affect the financial reporting of unpaid tax assessments. **Action taken:** During fiscal year 2012, we and IRS continued to identify misclassified unpaid assessments accounts resulting from IRS processing errors or delays. IRS compiled a report listing the misclassifications of account balances requiring corrections. However, IRS has not identified the underlying control deficiencies that impaired its ability to prevent or timely detect inaccuracies or errors in taxpayer accounts.	Open

---

[54]GAO, *Management Report: Improvements Are Needed in IRS's Internal Controls and Compliance with Laws and Regulations*, GAO-10-565R (Washington, D.C.: June 28, 2010).

ID no.	Recommendation	Status
10-04	Once IRS identifies the control weaknesses that result in inaccuracies or errors that materially affect the financial reporting of unpaid tax assessments, implement control procedures to routinely prevent, or to detect and correct, such errors. **Action taken:** During fiscal year 2012, we and IRS continued to identify misclassified unpaid assessments accounts that resulted in errors and inaccuracies in taxpayer accounts. IRS compiled a report listing the errors identified in its unpaid assessment estimation process. However, IRS has not yet identified the control weaknesses that resulted in these errors and has therefore not implemented corrective actions to routinely prevent, or detect and correct similar errors in taxpayer accounts.	Open
Controls Over Transmittal of Taxpayer Receipts and Information		
10-19	Establish procedures to track service center campus acknowledgments of unprocessable items with receipts. **Action taken:** In January 2012, IRS updated the *Lockbox Processing Guidelines* to require banks to retain all lockbox document transmittals and acknowledgments for a 1-year period. The banks are to have these documents available for review upon request. The update also requires the banks to call IRS if the faxed acknowledgment is not received by a specified time.	Closed
10-20	Establish procedures to monitor the process used by service center campuses and lockbox banks to acknowledge and track transmittals of unprocessable items with receipts. These procedures should include monitoring discrepancies and instituting appropriate corrective actions as needed. **Action taken:** During 2012, IRS revised its procedures for monitoring the process used by service center campuses and lockbox banks to acknowledge and track transmittals of unprocessable items with receipts by performing discretionary reviews, ad hoc unannounced reviews, or both, depending on each lockbox bank's performance. However, at all three of the service center campuses we visited during the fiscal year 2012 audit, we found that differences between the count of unprocessable items with remittances listed on the lockbox document transmittals were not always recorded on the lockbox data collection instrument.	Open

ID no.	Recommendation	Status
10-29	Analyze the various contractor access arrangements and establish a policy that requires security awareness training for all IRS contractors who are provided unescorted physical access to its facilities or taxpayer receipts and information. **Action taken:** During our fiscal year 2012 testing at all nine field offices and two of the service center campuses, we observed that contractors with staff-like access to IRS space were not required to receive security awareness training. IRS performed a risk assessment and identified contractors with unescorted workspace access (i.e. janitors, cleaning personnel, building maintenance personnel, and repair personnel) as posing a moderate risk, and has plans to require security awareness training for these contractors. We will continue to evaluate IRS's actions during our fiscal year 2013 audit.	Open

GAO-11-494R[55]

Controls over First-time Homebuyer Credit

11-01	Put procedures in place to periodically monitor the effectiveness of the new First-time Homebuyer Credit (FTHBC) validity checks for the duration of the filing of FTHBC claims to verify that they are working as intended. **Action taken:** IRS implemented procedures to review all unpostable transactions (including unpostable FTHBC returns) on a daily basis to ensure that validity checks are working as intended. During our fiscal year 2012 audit, we did not find any instances where IRS disbursed refunds on duplicate FTHBC claims.	Closed

Controls Over Manual Refunds

11-02	Establish a mechanism to enforce the existing requirement for appropriate managers to immediately notify the manual refund units of any personnel changes affecting the approval or processing of manual refunds. This may be accomplished through mechanisms such as issuing periodic alerts, providing training, having the manual refund unit perform quarterly validations of the list of manual refund approving officials, or a combination of these. **Action taken:** IRS implemented a quarterly process to update and validate personnel changes affecting the approval or processing of manual refunds. IRS updated the IRM with additional clarification on the quarterly process and on the use of a Manual Refund Signature Authorization Form, which IRS maintains for all employees authorized to approve manual refunds. Our testing during fiscal year 2012 did not identify any outdated lists of authorizing officials.	Closed

---

[55]GAO, *Management Report: Improvements Are Needed to Enhance the Internal Revenue Service's Internal Controls and Operating Effectiveness,* GAO-11-494R (Washington, D.C.: June 21, 2011).

ID no.	Recommendation	Status
Controls Over Purchases		
11-04	Establish formal written procedures requiring staff to review purchase contract terms against the goods and services received to date before requesting additional goods or services. **Action taken:** IRS plans to (1) issue an annual statement that addresses the basic requirements for awarding contracts and orders and (2) modify its policy to identify examples of unauthorized commitments, including failure to review existing limitations under contracts/blanket purchase agreements, failure to determine what services have already been performed or supplies delivered, or failure to seek an official interpretation of a contract's terms where doubt exists before placing an order by the contracting officer. Per IRS, the annual statement will also address the requirement to ensure the availability of funds before orders are placed. We will continue to monitor IRS's actions during our fiscal year 2013 audit.	Open
Controls Over Personnel Actions		
11-05	Establish procedures to centrally review and monitor the timeliness of personnel action requests and approvals to help ensure compliance with the Internal Revenue Manual and applicable Office of Personnel Management regulations and guidance. **Action taken:** Per IRS, as of September 2012, it completed the following actions: (1) issued clarifying guidance for personnel action requests (PAR), (2) established a centralized quality review program to monitor the timeliness of PARs, (3) developed new reports to assist in monitoring PAR timeliness, (4) finalized the closeout report and identified pain points within the process in order to aid in determining where to focus training and follow-up, (5) conducted training for human resource specialists on the newly implemented standardized PAR process, and (6) issued communications to managers to ensure PARs are initiated timely. In fiscal year 2013, IRS plans to provide detailed results on PAR actions to Human Resources-7, an executive human resource governance board, quarterly so the board can take action to significantly improve the number of PARs initiated timely by the business units. IRS reported that it will also reevaluate resources assigned to manage the PAR program to ensure timely processing is achievable based on workload and trends; communicate pay period results to employment offices leadership to better identify specific pain points within an office; and implement solutions and establish a stretch goal of timely PAR actions (excluding detail actions), which allows a margin of late actions because of unforeseen requests or issues (e.g., last-minute declinations and job offers, business unit changes/errors, and system glitches). We will continue to monitor IRS's actions during our fiscal year 2013 audit.	Open

ID no.	Recommendation	Status
Controls Over Contractor Access to Sensitive Information		
11-11	Perform a review of all existing contracts under $100,000 that (1) do not have an appointed contracting officer's technical representative and (2) do not require that contract employees obtain background investigations to assess whether the services performed under each contract warrant a requirement that contract employees obtain background investigations. **Action taken:** IRS's planned actions do not yet address the issues that gave rise to this recommendation. Specifically, the recommendation calls for a review of all contracts under $100,000 to determine if the contracts need to be modified to include additional background investigation requirements. However, IRS reported that because of the resource-intensive nature of such reviews and since a significant number of the initial set of contracts had expired, it has chosen to review only a sample of contracts. IRS plans to complete this review by June 2013. Given the potential risk related to this recommendation, it is possible that a sampling approach will not identify all contracts that should be modified to include additional background investigations.	Open
11-12	Based on a review of all existing contracts under $100,000 without an appointed contracting officer's technical representative that should require contract employees to obtain favorable background investigation results, amend those contracts to require that favorable background investigations be obtained for all relevant contract employees before routine, unescorted, unsupervised physical access to taxpayer information is granted. **Action taken:** By June 2013, IRS plans to modify contracts under $100,000 that are still active and have at least 6 months remaining in performance to require background investigations. However, IRS's approach to identifying these contracts, which is based on reviewing only a sample of contracts under $100,000, will not ensure that all contracts under $100,000 that should be modified will be modified.	Open

ID no.	Recommendation	Status
11-13	Establish a policy requiring collaborative oversight between IRS's key offices in determining whether potential service contracts involve routine, unescorted, unsupervised physical access to taxpayer information, thus requiring background investigations, regardless of contract award amount. This policy should include a process for the requiring business unit to communicate to the Office of Procurement and the Human Capital Office the services to be provided under the contract and any potential exposure of taxpayer information to contract employees providing the services, and for all three units to (1) evaluate the risk of exposure of taxpayer information prior to finalizing and awarding the contract and (2) ensure that the final contract requires favorable background investigations as applicable, commensurate with the assessed risk. **Action taken:** IRS is including the requirements of the Internal Revenue Service Acquisition Procedures 1052.204-9005, Submission of Security Forms and Related Materials, in new and existing contracts, as applicable. However, IRS has not yet established a policy requiring collaborative oversight between key offices in determining whether potential service contracts involve routine, unescorted, unsupervised physical access to taxpayer information, thus requiring background investigations, regardless of contract award amount. We will continue to evaluate IRS's actions during our fiscal year 2013 audit.	Open
Controls over Couriers		
11-14	Establish procedures to provide a consistent methodology for calculating and establishing allowable deposit courier trip time limits to be used by both service center campuses and lockbox banks that would assist in detecting potential unauthorized stops or other contractual violations by deposit couriers. Such procedures should include instructions for documenting and supporting how the trip limits were determined and require justification and approval for all established time limits that exceed the average trip time. **Action taken:** IRS reported that it is validating the procedures it established to provide a consistent methodology for calculating and establishing allowable deposit courier trip time limits to be used by service center campuses. Timeframes for delivering the deposit to the depository location that are listed in the courier contract Statement of Work will be reevaluated after analyzing information gathered during the annual unannounced internal security reviews that were completed from September 2012 through December 2012. IRS stated that it has stopped using deposit courier runs at the lockbox sites and no longer needs a methodology regarding courier times and lockbox banks because all lockbox sites now make daily deposits electronically through the use of the Electronic Check Presentment method. IRS plans to add the methodology used to determine courier timeframes for delivery of the deposits to IRM 3.8.45.1.9.7(3), *Headquarters Deposit Analyst Responsibility*, and to the courier statement of work by June 2013. We will continue to evaluate IRS's actions during our fiscal year 2013 audit.	Open

ID no.	Recommendation	Status
11-16	Enforce existing contractual requirements for the cargo doors of contract courier vehicles to be locked after picking up taxpayer information. **Action taken:** In February 2011, IRS distributed a reminder to the sub-contracting officer's representative and logistics chief in each territory regarding the contract requirements for secure transport. In April 2011, IRS implemented a monthly random review to ensure the contractors were meeting this requirement and the contractors also implemented their own internal review process. The results of IRS's random monthly reviews indicate that the contractors are complying with the requirements. However, during our fiscal year 2012 audit, we found that IRS did not apply these procedures to instances where contract couriers were making multiple stops at various business units. We will continue to monitor IRS's action during our fiscal year 2013 audit.	Open
11-17	Establish procedures to prevent or detect unauthorized access to taxpayer information in contract courier vehicles during transit. These procedures should detail specific activities to be performed by both the business unit sending and receiving the information transported by the contract courier. **Action taken:** IRS initiated a test at one Submission Processing Center in order to help establish procedures to prevent or detect unauthorized access to taxpayer information in contract courier vehicles during transit between all applicable IRS business unit locations. The test assessed the effectiveness of various methods for securing taxpayer information in transit between units and will continue through the first quarter of fiscal year 2013. By September 2013, IRS plans to implement procedures at other centers, as applicable, based on the test results. During our fiscal year 2012 audit, we found that while IRS established procedures directed at the Wage and Investment business unit to help prevent and detect unauthorized access to taxpayer information in contract courier vehicles, it did not have similar procedures for other IRS business units. In addition, these procedures did not provide additional safeguarding controls for instances where materials were left on the courier's vehicle for transport to another location. We will continue to evaluate IRS's actions during our fiscal year 2013 audit.	Open

ID no.	Recommendation	Status
11-18	Revise the guidance for conducting the periodic reviews of the contract couriers transporting taxpayer information from one IRS processing facility to another to include procedures for (1) physically verifying that courier vehicle cargo doors are locked after picking up this information and remain locked during transit to the final destination and (2) documenting the basis for the reviewer's conclusions. **Action taken:** IRS is continuing random monthly managerial reviews that it started in April 2011. These reviews indicate that the contractor is complying with the established requirements. In addition, the contractor has also implemented its own internal review process and documents and retains its review results. However, we found that IRS's guidance for conducting periodic reviews of the contract couriers transporting taxpayer information does not include the use of contract couriers transporting taxpayer information to non-Wage and Investment business units, nor does it take into account instances where contract couriers are making multiple stops to various business units. IRS initiated a test at one Submission Processing Center in order to help establish procedures to prevent or detect unauthorized access to taxpayer information in contract courier vehicles during transit between all applicable IRS business unit locations. By September 2013, IRS plans to implement procedures at other centers, as applicable, based on the test results. We will continue to evaluate IRS's actions during our fiscal year 2013 audit.	Open
Controls Over Physical Security - Lighting		
11-24	Revise the post orders for the service center campuses (SCC) and lockbox bank security guards to include specific procedures for timely reporting exterior lighting outages to SCC or lockbox bank facilities management. These procedures should specify (1) whom to contact to report lighting outages and (2) how to document and track lighting outages until resolved. **Action taken:** IRS updated *Lockbox Security Guidelines* to ensure officer post orders include exterior light outage(s) as an item that the guards must check. IRS updated the IRM to include specifically (1) whom to contact to report lighting outages and (2) how to document and track lighting outages until resolved. However, during our 2012 testing, we found that the post orders at two of the three SCCs we visited were not updated.	Open
11-25	Revise the nature and scope of the service center campuses' and lockbox banks' physical security reviews to include periodic after-dark assessments of physical security controls. **Action taken:** IRS stated that it is in the process of implementing a monitoring process through the Audit Management Checklist to review whether (1) guards are performing periodic after-dark assessments of physical security controls, (2) entries are being made in guard logs regarding exterior security checks, and (3) guards are properly reporting lighting outages in the routine physical security reviews of service center campuses. We will continue to evaluate IRS's actions during our fiscal year 2013 audit.	Open

ID no.	Recommendation	Status
Controls Over Property and Equipment Records		
11-26	Take steps to effectively implement the procedures requiring property staff to verify that the asset purchase price shown in the Asset Management Report agrees with the asset purchase price shown in the Integrated Financial System (IFS) and to resolve any variances before entering the information into the Information Technology Asset Management System. **Action taken:** In fiscal year 2011, IRS revised its operating procedures to require that property staff conduct research to ensure that the price of an asset on the Asset Management Report agrees with the price listed in IFS and resolve any variances before uploading an asset into its new property management system. During our fiscal year 2012 audit, we verified that procedures were effectively implemented.	Closed
GAO-12-683R[56]		
Controls Over Financial Reporting		
12-01	Establish and document an inventory of the specific systems involved in IRS's financial reporting process, including (1) describing what role each system plays in the financial reporting process; (2) concluding whether each system is considered to be material to financial reporting and why; and (3) denoting whether each system is controlled by IRS or by an external service provider and, if the latter, identifying the service provider. **Action taken:** By December 2013, IRS plans to modify its listing of systems involved in the financial reporting process to include (1) a description of the role each system plays; (2) whether the system is considered material to the financial statements; and (3) whether the system is controlled by IRS or by an external service provider and, if the latter, the name of the service provider.	Open

---

[56]GAO, *Management Report: Improvements Are Needed to Enhance the Internal Revenue Service's Internal Controls and Operating Effectiveness*, GAO-12-683R (Washington, D.C.: June 25, 2012).

ID no.	Recommendation	Status
12-02	Enhance existing policies and procedures pertaining to monitoring internal control over the automated systems operated by IRS personnel to specifically provide for routine, documented monitoring of the specific internal controls within its financial reporting systems that are intended to ensure the integrity of the data reported in the financial statements and other financial reports. This monitoring process should (1) involve both automated systems specialists and individuals with expertise in accounting and reporting, as appropriate, (2) encompass the specific automated internal controls that affect the authorizing, processing, transmitting, or reporting of material financial transactions, and (3) be designed to determine whether these internal controls are in place and operating effectively. **Action taken:** By December 2013, IRS plans to enhance existing policies and procedures to appropriately monitor internal control over the automated systems operated by IRS personnel that are identified as material to IRS's financial reporting process. The policies and procedures will be the basis for periodic and routine examinations of the financial systems that authorize, process, transmit, or report material financial transactions. These examinations will be conducted by multidisciplinary teams consisting of automated system specialists and accounting and reporting experts. By December 2013, IRS also plans to develop policies and procedures and use the financial systems monitoring process to determine whether these internal controls are in place and operating effectively.	Open
12-03	For any system identified as material to IRS's financial reporting process which is controlled by an external service provider, establish policies and procedures requiring and defining a routine, documented process for coordinating with the service provider to appropriately monitor related internal control. This may entail establishing an agreement with each service provider to allow IRS personnel access to either (1) the system concerned, as necessary to perform appropriate monitoring of internal control over financial reporting, or (2) periodic reports prepared in accordance with Statements on Standards for Attestation Engagements No. 16 documenting the results of monitoring performed by the service provider. **Action taken:** By December 2013, IRS plans to establish procedures for coordinating an internal control review with service providers of externally controlled financial systems that are identified as material to the financial statements.	Open

ID no.	Recommendation	Status
12-04	Establish policies and procedures with respect to any external financial reporting system IRS personnel themselves do not directly monitor that specify required steps to routinely review periodic reports prepared by service providers' auditors in accordance with Statements on Standards for Attestation Engagements (SSAE) No. 16, including steps to document (1) an assessment of whether a review's scope, methodology, and timing is appropriate to satisfy IRS's objectives; (2) any control deficiencies disclosed in the report, and an assessment of their materiality to IRS's financial reporting process and related risks; and (3) any compensating internal controls needed to mitigate any actual or potential effects of identified deficiencies upon IRS's internal and external financial reports resulting from any (a) material weakness, or (b) significant shortcoming in the scope, methodology, or timing of any SSAE No. 16 report reviewed relative to IRS's internal control objectives. **Action taken:** By December 2013, IRS plans to develop policies and procedures to document and routinely report on reviews of external providers' adherence to IRS's internal control objectives for any system identified as material to IRS's financial reporting process.	Open
Controls Over Accuracy of Tax Records		
12-05	Update IRS's procedures for comparing tax revenue recorded in the general ledger to detailed tax revenue transactions recorded in the master files to (1) establish minimum criteria defining a significant or unusual variance and (2) specify the steps required to effectively evaluate and resolve these variances. **Action taken:** IRS stated that in October 2012 it updated its revenue reconciliation desktop procedures for comparing tax revenue recorded in the general ledger to detailed tax revenue transactions recorded in the master files. The revised procedures established the minimum criteria for defining significant or unusual variances related to revenue and specify the steps required to effectively evaluate and resolve these variances. However, because IRS's actions were implemented after fiscal year 2012, we will evaluate them during our fiscal year 2013 audit.	Open
12-06	Update IRS's procedures for comparing tax revenue recorded in the general ledger to detailed tax revenue transactions recorded in the master files to require that management reviews ensure preparers evaluate and resolve unusual or significant variances. **Action taken:** IRS stated that in October 2012 it updated its revenue reconciliation desktop procedures to require a review and signoff by the manager or a management official to ensure that preparers evaluate and resolve significant or unusual variances. However, because these actions were implemented after fiscal year 2012, we will evaluate them during our fiscal year 2013 audit.	Open

ID no.	Recommendation	Status
Controls Over Reimbursable Revenue		
12-07	Establish and document procedures for ensuring that recorded reimbursable revenue, transfers in without reimbursement, and accounts receivable from the Department of the Treasury Forfeiture Fund (TFF) conform to federal accounting standards. **Action taken:** IRS developed, implemented and documented a direct charge reimbursable process for the TFF mandatory reimbursable program. During our fiscal year 2012 audit tests, we confirmed that IRS no longer recorded anticipated revenue for the TFF Mandatory program, but instead recorded actual revenue after the end of each month. However, it did not record or accrue revenue for the last month of the fiscal year, understating fiscal year 2012's revenues. The Chief Financial Officer organization is currently working with the Department of the Treasury to implement a new *U.S. Standard General Ledger* posting model in fiscal year 2013 for the two TFF discretionary programs (Super Surplus and Secretary's Enforcement).	Open
Controls Over Physical Security – Review Checklists		
12-08	Establish requirements specifying a required time frame for territory managers to perform the required review and approval of completed audit management checklists. **Action taken:** IRS updated the Audit Management Checklist Standard Operating Procedures to include the requirement that territory managers review and approve completed checklists within 30 days of the physical security specialist's signature date.	Closed
12-09	Establish procedures requiring Physical Security and Emergency Preparedness (PSEP) headquarters to centrally monitor compliance with the audit management checklist process to ensure that (1) PSEP analysts timely complete their physical security reviews using the proper audit management checklists and (2) territory managers timely review and properly document their reviews of completed audit management checklists. **Action taken:** IRS reported that in October 2012, it updated the Audit Management Checklist Standard Operating Procedures to require the Audit Management Program Office to perform reviews on a quarterly basis. The reviews will ensure that (1) territory offices complete the audit management checklist at campuses on a quarterly basis and at posts-of-duty on an annual basis using the most current checklist and (2) territory managers document their review and approval of completed checklists within 30 days of the physical security specialist's signature date. However, because IRS's actions were implemented after fiscal year 2012, we will assess these actions during our fiscal year 2013 audit.	Open

ID no.	Recommendation	Status
Controls Over Separation of Duties		
12-10	Update the Internal Revenue Manual (IRM) to specify steps to be followed to prevent campus support clerks as well as any other employees who process payments through the electronic check presentment system from making adjustments to taxpayer accounts. **Action taken:** IRS updated the IRM to require managers to use the Automated Command Code Access Control System to ensure that all employees who process payments through the electronic check presentment system have the appropriate command code restriction in their Integrated Data Retrieval System (IDRS) profile. However, during our fiscal year 2012 audit, we found several instances where IRS employees who had the capability to process paper checks electronically through the electronic check presentment system (Remittance Strategy for Paper Check Conversion) had access to sensitive IDRS command codes. IRS reported that it is analyzing the effect of the lack of segregation of duties in instances where staffing levels may not permit proper segregation of duties. By December 2014, IRS plans to identify appropriate actions to mitigate risks in the taxpayer assistance centers that exceed acceptable levels based on this analysis.	Open
Controls Over Net Cost Allocation		
12-11	Implement the September 2011 revised policy that requires an independent review of the rent check summary report to help ensure that the monthly rent allocation process is properly completed. **Action taken:** IRS implemented new procedures requiring an independent review of the rent check summary report. We did not note any discrepancies in IRS's monthly rent allocation process during our fiscal year 2012 testing.	Closed
12-12	Establish a policy requiring an independent review of changes made by the rent processing administrator to non-GSA lease data in the Graphic Database Interface system (GDI). **Action taken:** IRS updated its policy to require a review of non-General Services Administration (GSA) lease data in GDI to ensure that there are no unexpected changes. We did not identify any exceptions related to non-GSA lease data during our fiscal year 2012 testing.	Closed
12-13	Revise existing written procedures to require supervisory review of the Computer-Aided Facilities Management (CAFM) Quarterly Review Certifications and Statistics against the Graphic Database Interface system (GDI) validation walkthrough sheets. **Action taken:** IRS's revised procedures require supervisory review of the Quarterly Review Certifications against the GDI validation walkthrough sheets.	Closed

ID no.	Recommendation	Status
12-14	Establish mechanisms to monitor the implementation of and compliance with the revised policy established in October 2011 that requires field Computer-Aided Facilities Management (CAFM) program managers to maintain Graphic Database Interface system (GDI) Quarterly Review documentation, including GDI validation walkthrough sheets and GDI Quarterly Review certifications. **Action taken:** IRS's revised procedures require the GDI program analyst, the National CAFM program manager, or both, to compile each territory's submission of Quarterly Review documentation and to provide advice, consultation, and advocacy for the implementation of the revised policy requiring field CAFM program managers to maintain the Quarterly Review documentation. We did not identify any instances of missing or incomplete documentation during our fiscal year 2012 second quarter review of IRS's GDI Quarterly Review.	Closed
12-15	Establish mechanisms to monitor the implementation of and compliance with the revised policy established in October 2011 that defines the type of errors that should be captured on the Computer-Aided Facilities Management (CAFM) Quarterly Review Certifications to help ensure that field CAFM program managers consistently compile the errors found in their quarterly reviews for compilation in the overall CAFM Quarterly Review Statistics. **Action taken:** As part of IRS's annual GDI program review process, Real Estate and Facilities Management now conducts a formal review of error counts on the Quarterly Review Certifications to ensure that program managers consistently compile errors across various territories. Additionally, we did not identify any instances of CAFM program managers inconsistently compiling errors found in their fiscal year 2012 quarterly reviews.	Closed
Controls Over Leasehold Improvement Disposal Estimate		
12-16	Establish procedures to require the Office of Financial Reporting to ensure that extracted Graphic Database Interface system (GDI) data used to calculate the leasehold improvement disposal estimate is complete and accurate. **Action taken:** IRS revised the *Instructions for Calculating Leasehold Improvement Disposals* to include procedures requiring the Office of Financial Reporting to ensure that extracted GDI data used to calculate the disposal estimate is complete and accurate.	Closed
12-17	Implement the revised January 2012 procedures requiring comparison of the leases used in the prior year with the current year leases to help ensure that expired leases have not been extended and thus, are only counted once in the disposal estimates. **Action taken:** IRS implemented the revised January 2012 procedures requiring comparison of prior year leases with current year leases. During our fiscal year 2012 audit we validated that expired leases were not extended and were only counted once in the disposal estimate.	Closed

GAO-13-420R IRS Management Report

ID no.	Recommendation	Status
12-18	Implement the revised January 2012 procedures requiring preparation and review of leasehold improvement disposal calculations quarterly. **Action taken:** IRS implemented the revised January 2012 procedures requiring quarterly preparation and review of leasehold improvement calculations. During our fiscal year 2012 audit, we verified that the quarterly disposal calculations and the supporting documentation provided were reviewed.	Closed
Controls Over Purchases		
12-19	Provide training to contracting officers and contracting officer's technical representatives on their specific procedural requirements for obtaining and maintaining end user documentation of receipt and acceptance of the good or service prior to entering acknowledgement of receipt and acceptance in the procurement system. **Action taken:** IRS conducted receipt and acceptance training workshops in April 2012 for contracting officer's representatives. IRS's receipt and acceptance reference guides describe the required steps that users and managers must take to obtain and maintain end user documentation of receipt and acceptance. We did not identify any exceptions related to the lack of documentation of end user confirmation of goods/services during our fiscal year 2012 testing.	Closed
12-20	Establish a mechanism to periodically monitor contracting officers and contracting officer's technical representatives compliance with the requirement to obtain and document end user confirmation of receipt prior to entering receipt and acceptance into the procurement system. **Action taken:** IRS implemented a new process that requires staff from the Chief Financial Officer's office to perform an annual review of receipt and acceptance transactions to verify that contracting officer's representatives obtained and retained sufficient documentation of end user confirmation prior to inputting receipt and acceptance into the procurement system. During our fiscal year 2012 audit, we reviewed documentation from IRS's review and did not note any discrepancies.	Closed

ID no.	Recommendation	Status
Controls Over Patient Protection and Affordable Care Act Expenses		
12-21	Establish a mechanism for monitoring compliance with the existing requirement for employees and timekeepers to charge labor time spent on the Patient Protection and Affordable Care Act (PPACA) projects to the PPACA accounting code, such as through issuing periodic alerts, providing training and guidance, and/or having managers perform periodic reviews of employee labor time charges. **Action taken:** IRS established procedures for Corporate Budget to periodically monitor PPACA-related expenses. IRS's *FY 2012 Year-End Responsibilities and Cutoff Dates* instructions state that Corporate Budget will be monitoring PPACA charges and coordinating with business units to ensure that PPACA charges posted to direct accounts are moved to PPACA accounts prior to the fiscal year-end deadline. IRS also issued PPACA time charging guidance that outlines instructions for employees to record labor time worked on PPACA activities to the PPACA accounting code. We did not find any issues related to PPACA postings during our fiscal year 2012 audit.	Closed
12-22	Design and implement procedures specifying the review steps required to identify and research all transactions identified with a Patient Protection and Affordable Care Act (PPACA) internal order number in the agency's expense files to confirm that they are PPACA-related expenses and, if so, to ensure that they are charged to the PPACA appropriation where appropriate. **Action taken:** IRS established procedures designed to identify and research PPACA transactions in the agency's expense files and to transfer expenses as appropriate to the PPACA appropriation. During our fiscal year 2012 detail testing of both payroll and nonpayroll expenses, we did not identify any exceptions related to IRS charging PPACA expenses to an inappropriate appropriation.	Closed
Controls Over Time Card Approvals		
12-23	Revise the payroll standard operating procedures to specify steps that the human resource specialists are required to follow to ensure that each electronic time card is signed by an authorized official before the timecard is transmitted to the National Finance Center for processing and payment. **Action taken:** IRS updated its *DG-046 Desk Guide* with specific steps for human resource specialists to centrally monitor and resolve the Non-Validated Report, which identifies organizations with unsigned timecards, at the close of each pay cycle. Human resource specialists are responsible for following up with managers to ensure that all electronic time cards are signed by an authorized official before transmission to the National Finance Center.	Closed

ID no.	Recommendation	Status
12-24	Revise the payroll standard operating procedures to require that the designated proxy for a manager required to approve time cards be at an equivalent or higher level as the manager, consistent with the Internal Revenue Manual. **Action taken:** IRS has stated that it does not agree with this recommendation and does not plan to take further action. IRS stated that the execution of a proxy makes the approver equivalent to the initiator and therefore does not require that the designated proxy be at an equivalent or higher level than the employee's manager. As a result, a lower-level employee, who may have not had proper training, can be delegated as an acting supervisor for purposes of approving time cards. However, as discussed in our report (see GAO-12-683R), we believe that IRS's current procedures of delegating do not establish adequate internal control over the payroll approval process; are inconsistent with its own policies and delegation orders; and put IRS at increased risk of improperly paying employees, not meeting pay-related legal and regulatory requirements, and improperly accounting for payroll expenses.	Open
12-25	Incorporate in the planned 2012 policy change requiring the manager or designated proxy to sign the electronic time card before transmitting payroll records to the National Finance Center the requirement that the designated proxy be at an equivalent or higher level than the employee's manager. **Action taken:** IRS has stated that it does not agree with this recommendation and does not plan to take further action. IRS stated that the execution of a proxy makes the approver equivalent to the initiator and therefore does not require that the designated proxy be at an equivalent or higher level than the employee's manager. As a result, a lower-level employee, who may have not had proper training, can be delegated as an acting supervisor for purposes of approving time cards. However, as discussed in our report (see GAO-12-683R), we believe that IRS's current procedures of delegating do not establish adequate internal control over the payroll approval process; are inconsistent with its own policies and delegation orders; and put IRS at increased risk of improperly paying employees, not meeting pay-related legal and regulatory requirements, and improperly accounting for payroll expenses.	Open
12-26	Implement an edit control in IRS's time card system to identify and prevent the processing of timecards that have not been electronically signed. **Action taken:** Per IRS, it developed and implemented a new Single Entry Time Reporting (SETR) system functionality that requires electronic signatures for all timecards. IRS officials stated that this edit check, implemented in August 2012, now prevents SETR from transmitting unsigned time and attendance records to the National Finance Center. Managers are now required to review and electronically sign time and attendance records for all employees in SETR by the close of the pay period. However, IRS's actions were implemented late in the fiscal year subsequent to our testing. Thus, we will confirm in SETR whether the edit check effectively prevented the transmission of unsigned time and attendance records to the National Finance Center during our fiscal year 2013 audit.	Open

ID no.	Recommendation	Status
Controls Over Employee Pay Increases		
12-27	Remind managers of their responsibilities, procedures, and required time frames for either granting or denying a within-grade pay increase for employees with below fully successful ratings, such as by providing alerts in Human Resources Connect when a manager enters a less than fully successful rating or providing training to remind them of their responsibilities. **Action taken:** IRS issued procedures to remind managers of their responsibilities and required timeframes for granting or denying within-grade pay increases for employees with below fully successful ratings, and issued a Leaders' Alert to remind managers of their responsibilities and where to locate appropriate procedures.	Closed
12-28	Establish procedures for human resource specialists to track and monitor supervisory actions taken for employees with less than fully successful ratings that have a within-grade pay increase due date within 90 days to include specific required steps for following-up with managers to ensure the managers properly issue the employees a 60-day notification letter providing them an opportunity to improve their performance, make a timely determination on releasing or denying a within-grade pay increase, and properly carry out the requirements necessary to support the decision made. **Action taken:** IRS developed a matrix outlining steps for human resource specialists to take to remind the managers to properly issue a 60-day notification letter to each employee with a less than fully successful rating who is due a within-grade increase. The matrix also included the steps required for human resource specialists and Labor Relations to properly carry out the requirements necessary after a decision to deny or release the within-grade increase has been made. IRS stated that it also made revisions to Standard Operating Procedure 293-07, Rev. 3, to clarify and define steps for human resource specialists to assist managers in completing the process timely. However, neither the revised Standard Operating Procedure nor the matrix specifies what actions need to be taken by human resource specialists or Labor Relations if the managers do not respond to the reminders or do not make timely decisions on within-grade pay increases.	Open
12-29	Establish procedures for human resource specialists to track and monitor supervisory actions taken for employees with less than fully successful ratings that have a within-grade pay increase due date within 90 days to include specific required steps for timely granting a within-grade pay increase to such employees who were not given a 60-day notification letter. **Action taken:** IRS developed a matrix outlining steps for human resource specialists to take to remind managers to properly issue a 60-day notification letter to each employee with a less than fully successful rating who is due a within-grade increase. However, the matrix does not specify what actions need to be taken by human resource specialists to ensure that within-grade pay increases are timely granted to such employees who were not given a 60-day notification letter.	Open

ID no.	Recommendation	Status
Controls Over Payroll Transaction Errors		
12-30	Establish and document procedures for payroll staff to research and correct recycled errors from payroll processing on a regular and timely basis. **Action taken:** IRS has established the Error Correction Process requiring payroll analysts to research and make adjustments to correct recycled errors found during payroll processing every 2 weeks. Additionally, in the fourth quarter of fiscal year 2012, we found that the recycled error balance significantly decreased from the fiscal year 2011 balance.	Closed

Source: GAO.

Enclosure II: Comments from the Internal Revenue Service

DEPARTMENT OF THE TREASURY
INTERNAL REVENUE SERVICE
WASHINGTON, D.C. 20224

COMMISSIONER

April 26, 2013

Ms. Cheryl E. Clark
Director
Financial Management and Assurance
U.S. Government Accountability Office
441 G Street, NW
Washington, DC 20548

Dear Ms. Clark:

I am writing in response to the Government Accountability Office (GAO) draft report titled *Management Report: Improvements Are Needed to Enhance the IRS's Internal Controls (GAO-13-420R)*. We are pleased that GAO acknowledged our progress in addressing our financial management challenges and agreed to close 23 prior year financial management recommendations. We continue to make significant progress in addressing internal control deficiencies and financial management as evidenced by 13 consecutive years of clean audit opinions on our financial statements.

During fiscal year 2012, IRS strengthened controls over information security, refund disbursements, and release of federal tax liens. The enclosed response addresses each of your recommendations.

We are committed to implementing appropriate improvements to ensure that the IRS maintains sound financial management practices. If you have any questions, please contact me, or a member of your staff may contact Pamela LaRue, Chief Financial Officer, at (202) 622-6400.

Sincerely,

Steven T. Miller
Acting Commissioner

Enclosure

**GAO Recommendations and IRS Responses to
GAO FY 2012 Management Report
"Improvements Are Needed to Enhance
the Internal Revenue Service's Internal Controls"
GAO-13-420R**

Recommendation #1: We recommend that you direct the appropriate IRS officials, with respect to IRS's compensating statistical estimation process for unpaid tax assessments, to update the existing guidance for classifying and determining the dollar amount of individual unpaid assessments to provide additional guidance or specific procedures to follow when evaluating taxpayer accounts that involve complex legal and accounting interpretations. In updating the guidance, consider whether additional levels of management review should be performed on such complex cases.

Comments: The IRS agrees with this recommendation. In March 2013, the Chief Financial Officer (CFO) organization updated the existing guidance for classifying and determining the dollar amount of individual unpaid assessments to provide additional guidance to follow when evaluating taxpayer accounts that involve complex legal and accounting interpretations. The guidance includes additional levels of management review on complex cases.

Recommendation #2: We recommend that you direct the appropriate IRS officials, with respect to IRS's compensating statistical estimation process for unpaid tax assessments, to provide training on the new guidance to help staff evaluate and determine the proper accounting classification and amount of unpaid tax assessments, and to help with supervisory review of the sampled taxpayer accounts.

Comments: The IRS agrees with this recommendation. In March 2013, the CFO organization provided training on the new guidance to approve accounting classification.

Recommendation #3: We recommend that you direct the appropriate IRS officials to finalize implementation of the automated process for (1) routinely updating date of death information and deceased status in the master files using SSA data and (2) preventing automatic processing of a tax return submitted using a deceased taxpayer's social security number.

Comments: The IRS agrees with this recommendation. In January 2013, the Information Technology (IT) organization implemented programming to provide weekly updates to the Master File using data on dates of death provided by the Social Security Administration. The Master File updates cause any tax returns received under the decedent's Social Security Number, either as a primary or secondary taxpayer, to be diverted to the Error Resolution System where Tax Examiners review these returns to ensure any claims for refunds on behalf of decedents are appropriate.

Recommendation #4: We recommend that you direct the appropriate IRS officials to implement the policies and procedures that require the manual refund unit to verify (1) any manual refund signature authorization forms that are signed by a delegated official are accompanied by a designation to act form, and (2) the designation to act form is dated prior to the approval date on the manual refund signature authorization form.

Comments: The IRS agrees with this recommendation. In January 2013, the Wage & Investment (W&I) organization updated Internal Revenue Manual (IRM) 3.17.79.3.5, *Employees Authorized to Sign Requests for Refunds,* and implemented the revised procedures that require the manual refund unit to verify (1) any manual refund signature authorization forms that are signed by a delegated official are accompanied by a designation to act form, and (2) the designation to act form is dated prior to the approval date on the manual refund signature authorization form.

Recommendation #5: We recommend that you direct the appropriate IRS officials to perform a risk assessment to determine the appropriate level of IDRS access that should be granted to employee groups that handle hard-copy taxpayer receipts and related sensitive taxpayer information as part of their job responsibilities.

Comments: The IRS agrees with this recommendation. By October 2014, several W&I organizations and the IT organization will work jointly to perform a risk assessment to determine the appropriate level of Integrated Data Retrieval System (IDRS) access that should be granted to employees who handle hard-copy taxpayer receipts and related sensitive taxpayer information.

Recommendation #6: We recommend that you direct the appropriate IRS officials, based on the results of the risk assessment, to update the IRM accordingly to specify the appropriate level of IDRS access that should be allowed for (1) remittance perfection technicians and (2) all other employee groups with IDRS access that handle hard-copy taxpayer receipts and related sensitive information as part of their job responsibilities.

Comments: The IRS agrees with this recommendation. By December 2015, several W&I organizations and the IT organization will work jointly to update the applicable IRM sections to specify the appropriate level of IDRS access for employee groups with IDRS access, based on the results of the risk assessment.

Recommendation #7: We recommend that you direct the appropriate IRS officials to establish procedures to implement the updated IRM, including required steps to follow to prevent (1) remittance perfection technicians and (2) all other employee groups that handle hard-copy taxpayer receipts and related sensitive information as part of their job responsibilities from gaining access to command codes not required as part of their designated job duties.

Comments: The IRS agrees with this recommendation. By December 2015, as part of the risk assessment, several W&I organizations and the IT organization will evaluate existing controls that prevent employees from gaining access to command codes not required for their designated job duties, and will establish and document additional or replacement procedures as applicable.

Recommendation #8: We recommend that you direct the appropriate IRS officials to establish and implement written procedures to ensure that only costs are included in the cost allocation process.

Comments: The IRS agrees with this recommendation. By June 2013, the CFO organization will establish and implement written procedures to ensure that only costs are included in the cost allocation process.

Recommendation #9: We recommend that you direct the appropriate IRS officials to revise existing procedures to require staff responsible for monitoring the cost allocation to review the Presentation 1.1 report to determine if costs were fully allocated to the direct business units and, if not, to allocate the remaining costs.

Comments: The IRS agrees with this recommendation. By June 2013, the CFO organization will revise existing procedures to detail the review of Presentation 1.1 to include identifying that all costs are fully allocated at the operational business unit level.

Recommendation #10: We recommend that you direct the appropriate IRS officials to establish and implement written procedures to require that the Office of Cost Accounting inform the Debt Collection Unit of any changes to assigned functional area codes to be used for posting user fee transactions in IFS.

Comments: The IRS agrees with this recommendation. In November 2012, the CFO organization revised the User Fee procedures to require timely notification to the Debt Collection Unit of any changes to assigned functional area (FA) codes. In addition, in November 2012, the CFO established a procedure to provide an FA certification listing to the Debt Collection Unit annually.

Recommendation #11: We recommend that you direct the appropriate IRS officials to establish and implement written policies or procedures that require the agency to record the obligation of funds when a contract or agreement is entered into and prior to taking delivery of goods and services.

Comments: The IRS agrees with this recommendation. By August 2013, the CFO and the Agency-Wide Shared Services organizations will update existing policies and procedures to make it clear to all those involved in the acquisition process that the agency is required to timely record the obligation of funds.

Recommendation #12: We recommend that you direct the appropriate IRS officials to develop and implement a formal training program for staff assigned to perform and review excise tax certifications to include a comprehensive step-by-step description of the excise tax certification process.

Comments: The IRS agrees with this recommendation. By May 2013, the CFO organization will develop and implement formal training for all staff assigned to prepare and review the excise tax certifications, to include a comprehensive step-by-step description of the excise tax certification process.

Recommendation #13: We recommend that you direct the appropriate IRS officials to review existing supervisory review procedures to identify and implement additional needed actions to better ensure that certification errors do not continue to go undetected.

Comments: The IRS agrees with this recommendation. By May 2013, the CFO organization will implement expanded certification check sheets to enable a more comprehensive supervisory review and reduce the risk of certification errors.

Recommendation #14: We recommend that you direct the appropriate IRS officials to develop and implement written procedures requiring IRS to obtain documented concurrence from the other Treasury agencies involved in the excise tax collection and distribution process of any changes affecting how IRS calculates the amount of excise taxes it certifies to trust funds before IRS implements the change to its excise tax certification process.

Comments: The IRS agrees with this recommendation. By January 2014, the CFO organization will update IRM 1.31.3, *Procedures for the Certifications of Excise Tax Collections, Refunds and Credits*, to require IRS to obtain documented concurrence from affected Department of the Treasury organizations before implementing any changes to how IRS calculates the amount of excise taxes it certifies to the trust funds.

Enclosure III: GAO Contact and Staff Acknowledgments

GAO Contact: Cheryl E. Clark, (202) 512-9377 or clarkce@gao.gov.

Staff Acknowledgments	The following individuals made major contributions to this report: William J. Cordrey, Assistant Director; Doreen Eng, Assistant Director; Joshua Marcus, Auditor-in-Charge; Crystal Alfred; Sharon Byrd; Stephanie Chen; Nina Crocker; Melanie Darnell; Ryan Guthrie; Ted Hu; Tuan Lam; Delores Lee; Jenny Li; John Sawyer; Christopher Spain; Sunny Stanley; Chevalier Strong; and Gary Wiggins.

(196262)

GAO's Mission	The Government Accountability Office, the audit, evaluation, and investigative arm of Congress, exists to support Congress in meeting its constitutional responsibilities and to help improve the performance and accountability of the federal government for the American people. GAO examines the use of public funds; evaluates federal programs and policies; and provides analyses, recommendations, and other assistance to help Congress make informed oversight, policy, and funding decisions. GAO's commitment to good government is reflected in its core values of accountability, integrity, and reliability.
Obtaining Copies of GAO Reports and Testimony	The fastest and easiest way to obtain copies of GAO documents at no cost is through GAO's website (www.gao.gov). Each weekday afternoon, GAO posts on its website newly released reports, testimony, and correspondence. To have GAO e-mail you a list of newly posted products, go to www.gao.gov and select "E-mail Updates."
Order by Phone	The price of each GAO publication reflects GAO's actual cost of production and distribution and depends on the number of pages in the publication and whether the publication is printed in color or black and white. Pricing and ordering information is posted on GAO's website, http://www.gao.gov/ordering.htm.
	Place orders by calling (202) 512-6000, toll free (866) 801-7077, or TDD (202) 512-2537.
	Orders may be paid for using American Express, Discover Card, MasterCard, Visa, check, or money order. Call for additional information.
Connect with GAO	Connect with GAO on Facebook, Flickr, Twitter, and YouTube. Subscribe to our RSS Feeds or E-mail Updates. Listen to our Podcasts. Visit GAO on the web at www.gao.gov.
To Report Fraud, Waste, and Abuse in Federal Programs	Contact:
	Website: www.gao.gov/fraudnet/fraudnet.htm E-mail: fraudnet@gao.gov Automated answering system: (800) 424-5454 or (202) 512-7470
Congressional Relations	Katherine Siggerud, Managing Director, siggerudk@gao.gov, (202) 512-4400, U.S. Government Accountability Office, 441 G Street NW, Room 7125, Washington, DC 20548
Public Affairs	Chuck Young, Managing Director, youngc1@gao.gov, (202) 512-4800 U.S. Government Accountability Office, 441 G Street NW, Room 7149 Washington, DC 20548

www.ingramcontent.com/pod-product-compliance
Lightning Source LLC
Chambersburg PA
CBHW081117280526
45787CB00007B/2875